9ᵗʰ November 2000   19 years!!

I thought you could have a head start

♡ ↙ XXX

CHRISTMAS
COLLECTIBLES

CHRISTMAS COLLECTIBLES

A GUIDE TO SELECTING, COLLECTING, AND ENJOYING THE TREASURES OF CHRISTMAS PAST

LISSA AND DICK SMITH

THE APPLE PRESS

Dedication:
For Kendra, who
always loved Christmas

A QUINTET BOOK

Published by The Apple Press
6 Blundell Street
London N7 9BH

ISBN 1–85076–430–1

This book was designed and produced by
Quintet Publishing Limited
6 Blundell Street
London N7 9BH

Creative Director: Richard Dewing
Designer: Peter Laws
Consultant Editor: Maria von Staufer
Project Editor: Katie Preston
Editor: Maggi McCormick
Photographer: Harry Rinker Jr.

Typeset in Great Britain by
Central Southern Typesetters, Eastbourne
Manufactured in Singapore by Eray Scan Pte. Limited
Printed in Hong Kong by Leefung-Asco Printers Limited

Contents

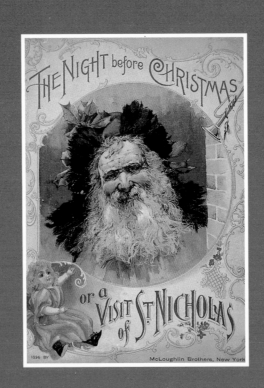

The Night before Christmas

or a Visit of St. Nicholas

1896 BY McLoughlin Brothers, New York

CHAPTER ONE

The History of Christmas

Christmas, Weihnacht, Yule, Noel and "the Holidays" all suggest a season of magic, peace and miracles – the Christmas we know today. How did we arrive at this concept of Christmas?

The central theme of Christmas is the birth of Christ. The stories from the Bible of the angels, shepherds and Wisemen are prominent in our carols, decorations and pageants. The Bethlehem Christmas was a religious observance without the trappings and festivities later associated with the holiday.

THE ORIGINS OF CHRISTMAS

Many aspects of contemporary Christmas have their roots in Pre-Christian celebrations from a number of countries and cultures. From the Romans came the Saturnalia to honour the early god, Saturn. From 17 December to 24 December, public gathering places were decorated with flowers, gifts and candles were purchased and exchanged, and the population – slaves and masters alike – celebrated with feasts and merriment.

LEFT
A decorated feather tree from the early 20th century.

LEFT
*Elaborate Nativity
display (c. 1910).
Figures in a variety of
materials and styles,
ranging from
composition dolls to wax
angels, illustrate what
was available in the early
20th century.*

As Roman culture spread through Europe, other festivals occurring at this time of year became associated with Christmas. In Scandinavia, a period of festivities known as Yule contributed another impetus to celebration as opposed to spirituality. As winter ended the growing season, the need to utilize summer's bounty encouraged massive feasting.

Celtic culture of the British Isles revered all green plants, but particularly evergreens, mistletoe, and holly. These greens were important symbols of fertility and were used for medicinal purposes. Celts decorated their homes and altars with their boughs.

New Christmas customs appeared in the Middle Ages. The most prominent contribution was the carol. By the 14th century, carols were associated with the religious observance of Christ's birth. They lacked the formality of traditional church music, since they were written by parish poets, minstrels and balladeers.

In Italy began the tradition of the re-enactment of the birth of Christ and the construction of scenes of the Nativity. It is said that St Francis, as part of his efforts to bring spiritual knowledge to the laity, directed a realistic enactment of the first Christmas, and the observance spread throughout Italy and Europe.

Days honouring saints have contributed to our Christmas celebrations. A prominent figure in today's Christmas is St Nicholas

who for centuries has been honoured on 6 December. He was one of the forerunners of Santa Claus.

In parts of Europe, the Festival of Lights, St Lucia's Day, 13 December, ushered in the holiday season. In Sweden, the prettiest girl in the house wears a white dress, red sash, and a crown of lighted candles and leads a procession through the house prior to the breakfast feast. In Italy, the day is celebrated with torchlight processions. In parts of Europe St Lucia is to girls what St Nicholas is to boys. The practice of putting lighted candles in windows is an outcome of this festival.

Another popular European ritual was the burning of the Yule Log. Although the custom had regional variations, the Log usually was associated with magical or spiritual powers. The Yule Log is strongly embedded in the pagan worship of vegetation and fire. The burning of the Log is still popular in parts of Europe and the United States.

CHRISTMAS GIFT-GIVING

The contemporary emphasis on materialism and gift-giving has been with us since the beginning of any celebration resembling Christmas. Gift-giving and excess in the season of Saturnalia were decried by ancient authors.

The Celtic culture added further emphasis to the practice of gift-giving. Prominent Celts sponsored massive feasts which included giving away possessions. This practice led to a constant redistribution of wealth, which helped to maintain a relatively level society. In recent centuries, gift-giving continued to be popular in festivities that surround Christmas. The feast-days of St Nicholas and St Lucia highlighted the giving of gifts to children.

The bearing of gifts cannot be discussed without mentioning the three Kings that carried gifts to the baby Jesus in Bethlehem. Their reverence and generosity is considered by many to be the basis for our gift-giving. In the Western Church this event is celebrated on 6 January – Epiphany.

Celebrating Christmas has been controversial since its inception. Since numerous Christmas festivities found their roots in pagan practices, they were an easy target for Church conservatives. The feasting, gift-giving, and frequent excess presented a drastic variance from the simplicity of the Nativity, and many people throughout the centuries, and into the present, condemn such "extravagant" practices.

The Reformation and the rise of basic-thinking Protestant groups emphasized the conflict between the secular and religious observance of Christmas. As these "plain" sects emigrated to America, Christmas celebrations were discouraged or banned outright in the New World.

ABOVE
Santa Claus gives his blessing to some Christmas revellers.

*Victorian toys and
games. By the middle of
the 19th century,
children's entertainment
had become a major
industry. Here are a few
examples of the wide
variety produced in many
countries. (Clockwise) A
German bisque doll
holding an American
cloth doll sitting in a
wicker rocker; an
American lithographed
"Fish Pond" game box; a
wooden ark with
lithographed paper Noah
and wife; a German
sheep pull toy; the "Fish
Pond" game; a brightly
lithographed soldiers
book from Germany; a
German horse pull toy; a
German castle; a British
colour-lithographed
children's travel book;
and a straw-stuffed bear
of unknown origin.*

RIGHT
This photograph from 1897 illustrates the pre-nursery-grown Christmas tree and a variety of children's and dolls' furniture. This little girl and her bounty reflect the Victorians' devotion to their offspring.

LEFT
A school Christmas pageant. The large trees, supported by wooden stands, display an exceptional collection of ornaments. The girls are all dressed in angelic white and some are carrying flags and stars from their Christmas programme.

THE SOUNDS OF CHRISTMAS

No discussion of Christmas traditions is complete without mentioning noise. The revelry of Saturnalia and the carousing of the Celts set a standard for holiday cacophony. Add horns, drums, noisemakers and cheers, and the roar of the celebration becomes deafening. Then the introduction of gunpowder allowed the celebration to include fireworks and groups parading while firing their guns. Today most of the "noise" has moved to New Year's Day; but Christmas target shoots and parades are still popular in regions of Europe and the southern United States.

VICTORIAN TRADITIONS

The traditions connected with our contemporary Christmas began in the reign of Britain's Queen Victoria. This period is known for its lavish interiors and architecture and dedication to the family, especially children. Victorian homes were by today's standards ornate and filled with objects. These values and styles forever changed the Christmas holiday.

Victorian embellishment of the holiday resulted in a significant increase in the creation and manufacture of decorations. Homes were adorned inside and out with garlands, wreaths and commercially available items.

In German tradition, a candlelit fir tree hung with fruit and gifts was a traditional part of the Christmas celebration. In the Victorian era, the popularity of the evergreen Christmas tree spread beyond its origins. To suit the times, more and more decorations were devised and industries developed for the manufacture of glass, paper and cotton ornaments, strings of glass beads and figural sweet containers.

Industrialization and a rising standard of living, combined with the emphasis on family life, created another manufacturing opportunity – children's toys and games. Many Victorians had the luxury of both time and money to lavish on their children in the form of gifts, clothing and parties.

Santa Claus became a symbol of gift-giving. The legends that surrounded this jolly elf were embraced by the populace and he rapidly became the icon for a commercial and secular holiday.

In spite of the increased commercialization, Christmas continued to be a major religious celebration. Churches were decorated with trees and greenery. Pageants that showcased children performing plays and recitations were staged. Churches continued

25 DECEMBER – WHY?

The early Christian church placed no emphasis on the time of Christ's birth. The first event of importance in the life of Christ was his baptism in the River Jordan on 6 January. In early times, this baptism was considered the beginning of Christ's divinity, and a feast day, Epiphany, developed on this date in the Eastern Church.

During the 4th century AD, the church in Rome declared 25 December as the official day of celebration of Christ's Nativity. It is not definitively known why this particular date was chosen. Nothing in the Bible indicates a specific time of year, and some scholars argue that a winter date is not appropriate: Rome would not have ordered a census at a time of year when travel was difficult, and the likelihood that shepherds would have been tending their flocks in the fields during winter is remote.

In the Julian Calendar 25 December marked the winter solstice, which associated a Nativity on that date with the rebirth of the sun. Another speculation is that the religion of Mithraism was a serious rival to Christianity, and its worship of the sun was appropriated by the church fathers.

Gradually 25 December became universally accepted by most of the Western world, but 6 January remains the feast day of the Nativity in Eastern Orthodox Churches.

RIGHT

Carolling and music are an integral part of the Christmas holiday. This copy of the 1907 sheet music of "Silver Sleigh Bells" highlights the worldwide distribution of Christmas goods. The bright colours and charming picture were designed to entrance the holiday consumer.

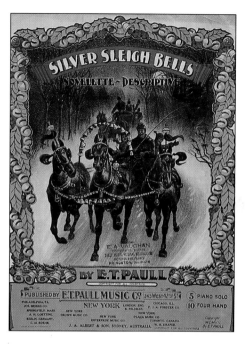

the medieval practice of re-enacting the Nativity.

The 14th-century observance of Christ's birth through carolling continued to grow through the years. By the Victorian era there was a large body of religious Christmas music. The increasing secular emphasis of the holiday gave rise to popular Christmas music and this trend continues today.

The Christmas menu of observances grows longer every year. Each culture contributes a portion of their holiday, which is then widely accepted. Families develop their own traditions and the expanding generations cement them into rituals.

This holiday has bequeathed us many relics. Those who cherish Christmases past enjoy searching for these treasures and look forward to December when they all may be displayed.

CHAPTER TWO

The Changing Image of Santa Claus

t Nicholas, Sinterklaas, Christkindl, Kris Kringle, Father Christmas and Pelz-Nicol are all manifestations of the gift-giver, Santa Claus. Like Christmas itself, the mystical Santa Claus is a combination of customs and practices of many cultures.

The legend of our modern Santa began around the 4th century in Asia Minor. Here, in Myra of Lycia, Bishop Nicholas became renowned for exceptional acts of generosity and kindness and St Nicholas became the patron of children, marriageable maidens, sailors and Russia.

The feast day of St Nicholas is on 6 December. Small gifts for children appeared on this day in households that honoured the goodly saint. Christmas was also celebrated by many of these families, but they were two separate holidays. Some countries in Europe still commemorate St Nicholas on his feast day.

The earliest "Santa Claus" was St. Nicholas dressed in a bishop's mitre and robe, and carrying a staff. His face was usually depicted as kindly and bearded. Adults dressed in his attire made visits to homes to enquire about the behaviour of children. Before

RIGHT
A woodcut from the Middle Ages depicting the legend of St. Nicholas' healing powers.

ABOVE

A 15th-century painting by Lorenzo di Bicci — one of the earliest representations of St Nicholas delivering presents.

the children went to bed, they placed their shoes outside the door and the next morning they happily retrieved their shoes heaped with goodies.

The growth of Protestantism decreased the emphasis on saints and increased the importance of the Christ Child.

In German provinces the Christ Child or Christkind or Christkindl was credited as the bringer of presents the children received on Christmas Eve.

A pagan corruption of the Christkindl visitation is Knecht Rupert, a strange figure dressed in animal skins and straw, who interrogates children about their catechism. This character rewarded the good children with sweets and punished the bad children. A similar German Christmas Eve visitor was Pelznichel. He was a dark version of St Nicholas, who also dressed in furs and carried switches for punishing the naughty and a bag of treats for rewarding the good.

St Nicholas visited the children in Austria, too, but here he appeared on Christmas Eve. He was still dressed in bishop-like clothing, but he was now travelling with "Ruprecht", a terrifying animal-person that persuaded the children to be virtuous.

An Anglo-Saxon addition to the Christmas figure was Father Christmas. He was a combination of St Nicholas, Saturn and Thor. This character was often pictured in fur robes trimmed with holly and ivy. Father Christmas was more boisterous and jovial than his mainland counterparts. He carried switches to threaten the bad and a bag of toys to reward the deserving.

While the Santa legends have traditionally been male figures, there are female gift-givers. In Russia a character known as Kolyada – a pagan deity – and Baboushka – a legendary story character – travel from house to house distributing gifts. Regions of Italy also celebrate a female gift-giver, Befana. This "witch"

ABOVE
A Dutch St. Nicholas and his assistant, Peter, cross the rooftops to deliver gifts.

descends chimneys and is often pictured with a broom.

The Dutch interpretation of St Nicholas, Sinterklaas; the Germanic St Nicholas, Pelznichel; Father Christmas and the Christkindl all emigrated to America. The Dutch colonists were the major importers of the magical gift-giver. Prior to their arrival in the New World, the earlier Puritans reviled Christmas festivities and Santa figures.

The Dutch Christmas Eve gift-giver wore a red coat, carried a sack of gifts, travelled on an animal and had the name "Sinter-klaas", which was easily Anglicized into Santa Claus. Sinterklaas left treats and toys in shoes or stockings that were placed near the hearth or on the mantel. The Dutch settlers pictured a tall, reedy figure with a rather austere expression, much like the one in Holland.

Santa's image was clarified by Clement Moore in 1823 with his composition *A Visit from St. Nicholas.* Dr Moore modified Mr Irving's wagon to a sleigh, added eight reindeer with names and gave us a full picture of Santa's appearance. Dr Moore also immortalized a "sleigh full of toys" and the fact that Santa arrived by dropping down the chimney.

RIGHT
*An image of Santa Claus
as both punisher and
gift-giver.*

Washington Irving in his 1809 book, *Knickerbocker's History of New York from the Beginning of the World to the End of the Dutch Dynasty,* relates a detailed description of Sinterklaas. His contributions to our modern Santa's appearance were a hat, hose, and a long-stemmed pipe. His jolly St Nick flew over rooftops in a wagon, brought presents to children via the chimney, laid a finger beside his nose and was known to wink. Sound familiar?

From Washington Irving's
Knickerbocker's History of New York.

"... a goodly image of St. Nicholas, equipped with a low, broad-brimmed hat, a huge pair of Flemish trunk-hose, and a pipe ..."

"... and lo, the good St. Nicholas came riding over the tops of the trees, in that selfsame wagon wherein he brings his yearly presents to children ..."

"... knew him by his broad hat, his long pipe, and the resemblance which he bore to the figure on the bow of the Goede Vrouw ..."

"... he never shows us the light of his countenance, nor ever visits us, save one night in the year; when he rattles down the chimneys ... confining his presents merely to the children ...'"

"... and when St. Nicholas had smoked his pipe, he twisted it in his hatband, and laying his finger beside his nose, gave the astonished Van Kortlandt a very significant wink, then mounting his wagon, he returned over the tree-tops and disappeared ..."

"... the good St. Nicholas would often make his appearance in his beloved city, of a holiday afternoon, riding jollily among the tree-tops, or over the roofs of the houses, now and then drawing forth magnificent presents from his breeches pockets, and dropping them down the chimneys ..."

From Clement Moore's

An Account of a Visit from St. Nicholas

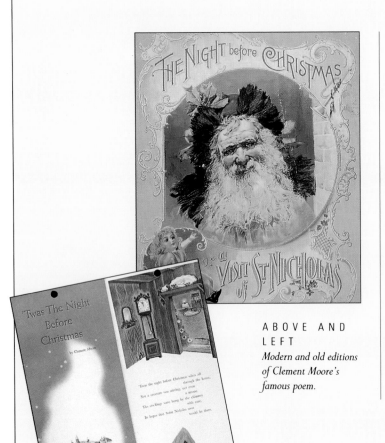

ABOVE AND LEFT
Modern and old editions of Clement Moore's famous poem.

". . . a little old driver so lively and quick, . . ."

"He was dressed all in fur, from his head to his foot,

And his clothes were all tarnished with ashes and soot;

A bundle of Toys he had flung on his back,

And he look'd like a peddler just opening his pack.

His eyes – how they twinkled! His dimples how merry!

His cheeks were like roses, his nose like a cherry.

His droll little mouth was drawn up like a bow,

And the beard on his chin was as white as the snow.

The stump of a pipe he held tight in his teeth,

And the smoke it encircled his head like a wreath.

He had a broad face and a little round belly,

That shook, when he laughed, like a bowl full of jelly.

He was chubby and plump, a right jolly old elf, . . ."

The next "Santa" landmark contributor is Thomas Nast, a Bavarian immigrant. Mr Nast was a political cartoonist for *Harper's Weekly* who rose to popularity through his daring satirical drawings that exposed corruption in American politics. He drew his first Santa Claus in the early 1860s and contributed more than twenty additional images on a yearly basis. Mr Nast's sketches were predominantly black and white, but he produced a series of colour illustrations for a children's publisher.

Santa continued to be elfin in stature while growing in breadth. He still sported the "Father Christmas" crown of holly on his hat and often was garbed in the long "St Nicholas" red robe now trimmed in ermine. A trademark of Nast's Santa was the long clay pipe of the Dutch Sinterklaas.

The American Santa of the 19th century was invariably a jolly and kindly gentleman with none of the stern features of the German Pelznichel. Santa was white-haired and had a long white beard and moustache. This appearance is today so strongly identified with Santa Claus that a man with a white beard and moustache is usually nicknamed "Santa". His face is now overly chubby with a ruddy complexion, probably due to his life in the cold and obvious overindulgence at the dining table.

The final milepost in the development of our present-day Santa was the result of commercialization and communication. In America Santa Claus became the central figure in the holiday advertising of the Coca-Cola Bottling Company. Their artist,

Probably Mr Nast's greatest gift to our character was to make him a believable per on. He rounded out St Nick by giving him a home, a workshop, and the arduous task of maintaining a vigilant eye on the year-round behaviour of the world's children. In addition, he now had a permanent address. The North Pole!

ABOVE AND
LEFT
*The archetypal Santa
Claus image developed by
Haddon Sundblom for
the Coca-Cola
advertising campaign in
the US.*

LEFT
These Father Christmas figures were made in Germany from 1880 to 1910, with the exception of the small blue-robed figure in the front. This Father Christmas is an example of an early Pennsylvania "Santa Claus".

Haddon Sundblom, created an adult who enshrined Nast's face and costume. The Santa Coca-Cola campaign continued for more than forty years and perpetuated customs from all over the world. Some of his more memorable images are: hanging the stockings on the chimney, leaving biscuits and milk for Santa and carrots for the reindeer, and building toys with his elves. This Sundblom-Coke Santa was such a success that it created a universally accepted Santa Claus image.

DECORATIVE SANTAS

The Victorian penchant for adornment triggered a demand for commercial ornamentation and the Germans rose to the challenge. The majority of the toys in the world were already produced in Germany, consequently it was a natural step to manufacture Christmas decorations. The fabricated Santas experienced the same image modifications that the Santa legends encountered.

The oldest readily available Santa images are German hollow-moulded papier-mâché with plaster overlay. These Father Christmases or Belsnickels (a corruption of Pelznichel) follow the traditional St Nicholas image. The figures are fierce of face, wear a long robe and have a peaked hood frequently trimmed in chenille. They carry a bundle of switches, a goose-feather tree, or a sprig of Erikamoos (dried heather). The faces of these figures are finely moulded, delicately painted, and have a distinctively curved eyebrow. The "Santas" routinely have folded arms with the hands tucked in the sleeves and wear tall black boots moulded into a

Early German representations (1900 to 1920) of Santa Claus. (Left to right) Composition Santa, with a cotton flannel coat and a rabbit fur beard, carrying a feather tree; this Santa is marching on a wooden mica-covered board with a basket of toys on his back. The next figure straddles a wooden sled; a pop-up chimney is the home of this cotton-bearded Santa. The last figure is a sweet box.

Early Japanese Santas produced from 1920 to 1950. All the figures are mounted on white cardboard discs. Their jackets are made of red flannel or red-flocked paper, and they are belted with oilcloth. Santa's hands are made of cotton batting and they hold a variety of items such as bells, candles, Erikamoos trees and bags. The Santa second from the left has a crepe paper boa around his neck.

base. Their long robes are white, red, yellow, green, blue, purple, pink, brown, or black and are highlighted with mica or gold flakes. (The colours are listed in order, common to rare.)

The German Belsnickels or Santa figures were produced from around 1880 to 1910 in a large variety of sizes from 5cm (2in) tree ornaments to 60cm (24in) statues. Some, which separate between the base of the coat and the top of the boots, were used as sweet containers.

These Father Christmas images enjoyed great popularity. Surviving ones have been treasured for many years and are handed down from generation to generation within families.

Germany continued to be preeminent in the creation of "Santa" likeness, and during the first three decades of the 20th

century, the appearance of Christmas men begin to look more like Santa Claus. They vary in concept from stern adults to merry elves.

Many figures of this period have a composition body of a roughly textured amalgamation of sawdust, glue, paper, plaster and straw. The Santas are often hump-backed, with either red, green, white or purple coats. The cloth is velvet or flannel. Their trousers of blue or black are tucked into painted black boots.

The faces of these characters, while not as finely moulded or as delicately painted as the Belsnickels, still show considerable attention to detail and a decided effort to display a distinctive personality. This personality can range from a thin austere countenance to a jolly, plump and red-cheeked expression. These

gentlemen continued to have moustaches and beards which were fabricated from white rabbit fur.

Figures of this time are engaged in a variety of activities and placed in many different settings. They are found holding a feather tree, a bunch of switches, a bag of toys, or a walking stick. Occasionally a basket or a bag is strapped to their backs. They are perched on logs or stumps and in pop-up chimneys, and are standing on mica-covered boards. Their activities include driving moss carts, cars and one-reindeer sleighs, and riding bicycles, skiing, striding and riding on reindeer.

Japan also produced composition figures. The difference between the two countries' handiwork is apparent when the two appear side by side. The Japanese faces are very pink, and the

Japanese celluloid Santas (1920 to 1940). (Left to right) 7.5cm (3in) Santa holding a pack with a tennis racket, one-piece Santa sleigh, and reindeer. 15cm (6in) and 7.5cm (3in) Santas holding dolls behind their backs. 2.5cm (1in) tall Santa sleigh and deer fabricated from three different pieces. Santa in a seashell-shaped sleigh pulled by a reindeer. The figure on the far right is a small Santa waving with a pack on his back.

American celluloid Santas marked Irwin (1920 to 1940). (Left to right) Small one-piece moulded Santa, sleigh and reindeer. 10cm (4in) rotund Santa. 5cm (2in) tree ornament. 15cm (6in) Santa with a long coat. 7.5cm (3in) Santa perched on a block. Small "Father Christmas". 5cm (2in) solid red Santa. Santa on metal skis with wooden poles. Finally, small Santa in a chimney.

At the turn of the century, Germany manufactured celluloid Christmas Men, but Japan and the United States dominated the market by the 1920s. The process of moulding celluloid created many different styles and shapes. Santa can be discovered driving a car, riding in a hot-air balloon, guiding a sleigh, pedalling a bicycle, gliding on skis, or sitting in the middle of a carousel.

LEFT
Chenille and bisque
Santas. (Left to right)
Japanese chenille Santa
with a moulded paper
head (1930s). 2.5cm
(1in) Japanese bisque
Santa (1930s). Two
7.5cm (3in) Japanese
bisque Santas with long
coats (1930s). 2.5cm
(1in) Japanese bisque
Santa, usually perched

on a sweet (1930s).
White Japanese chenille
Santa ornament with a
composition face
(1930s). American
bisque Santa Claus
(1950s). Another
Japanese bisque sweet
topper (1930s). An
American red chenille
Santa with a foil face
and cotton beard
(1940s).

facial features are crude in detail. They have red flannel or cotton jackets that over time have faded to a soft shade reminiscent of tomato soup. Their trousers are blue and their boots are black. The majority of these Santas sport an oilcloth belt across their trim waistline. The Japanese composition characters are engaged in many of the same activities and posed in similar ways to the German ones. Some of these Santas have composition faces and bodies of bundled straw.

Germany and Japan produced another type of Santa Claus made of cotton batting. These figures commonly had composition faces with cotton beards. German fellows frequently had die-cut faces, hands and legs. Ranging in size from 5–25cm (2–10in), they are found both in soft cotton and hard-formed.

Germany and Japan also split the bisque Santa market. Most of the bisque figures qualify as cake decorations and were created in at least 50 different poses. The primary difference in the two countries' products is the detail in the German moulds. Japan made a particularly interesting set of Santa and his elves.

WHAT IS CELLULOID?

Celluloid was developed in England and was first used for manufacturing in 1869 in Newark, New Jersey. Germany was the first to use celluloid for toys and Christmas items. Rheinische Gummi und Celluloid Fabrik, a company in Mannheim, marked their celluloid products with a turtle. The Irwin Company was a large American manufacturer. Celluloid was an early "plastic" made from raw cotton treated with nitric acid. The cellulose nitrate pulp was then mixed with camphor gum and formed into sheets. Heated, this material could be easily moulded. While advertised as unbreakable, celluloid items were easily dented and split along the seams. Celluloid is also extremely flammable and distorted by heat.

Celluloid had its heyday between 1920 and 1940 and was last produced around 1950. World War II played a major role in the demise of celluloid consumer products because the raw materials were needed for the war effort.

ABOVE

Chalk santas. The large American Santa bank was a carnival giveaway and has a chiselled hole in the back (late 1940s to the early 1950s). (Front row, left to right) American Santa face candleholder (1930s). American Santa. The next three Santas are stamped "England" on their bases and the last Santa was made in the United States; his pack has a hole for a candle.

ABOVE RIGHT

American pressed cardboard Santas (1920s to 1950s). These Santas were probably purchased as decorative items rather than sweet containers, although the large white Santa in back is holding a net sack that reaches down his back. He has a label inside his base marked "Harry and David – Medford, Oregon" and his sack most likely held assorted nuts and sweets. The red Santa to his right has a pack on his back that is marked in ink – "Junior, January 8, 1927".

LEFT

American pressed cardboard Santas, produced from the 1920s to the 1940s. All the Santas have open packs that were used as sweet containers.

American glass sweet containers manufactured by the Victory Co. or in Jeanette, Pennsylvania, USA. (Left to right) The first two figures and the last all have metal screw-on bases (1930s). The Santa second from the right has a hard plastic head that twists off to dispense the sweets (late 1940s to 1950s). The two Santas on the right are also banks.

Commonly known as "chalk", but in reality ordinary casting plaster has been a familiar medium for Santa Claus creators. Early chalk Father Christmas figures which had a traditional "St Nicholas" appearance were made in German-American communities. England produced a series of miniature Santa Men in chalk, used as cake decorations, that are still popular. Chalk continued to be used for a variety of Santa representations from cups to candleholders, with large numbers produced from 1940 to 1950.

Pressed and moulded cardboard figures were produced primarily in the United States between the 1930s and the 1950s. These men appeared in various stances and were basically red or white. Because of their original low cost and ample size, as well as their appealing personality, these Santas were produced in large numbers and are frequently found in shops and auctions.

The U.S. dominated the field in glass sweet containers. A variety of different glass Santas with metal lids were used by the Victory Candy Company. In addition, glass Santas were produced for holding perfume.

Metal in the form of iron, white metal and tin has been used for Santas throughout the history of Christmas decorations. Cast-iron Santas, sleighs and reindeer are among the earliest and rarest images. Soft or white metal, which was easily moulded, was frequently utilized for coin banks and assorted advertising and giveaway Christmas figures.

Tin is also a popular medium. Early tin figures were painted with a lacquer coating, which added colour while protecting the

LEFT

Japanese wind-up toys (1950 to 1960). The three to the rear are made of metal covered with cotton flannel, and have cotton beards. The Santa on the reindeer has a metal body and a plastic head; his reindeer has a metal body covered with material, and hops when the toy is wound up. The Santa on the left pulls a present out of his pack when wound. The next Santa flips the pages of an alphabet book. The last Santa rings a bell and waves celluloid balloons.

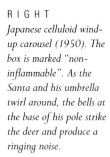

RIGHT

Japanese celluloid wind-up carousel (1950). The box is marked "non-inflammable". As the Santa and his umbrella twirl around, the bells at the base of his pole strike the deer and produce a ringing noise.

tin from rust. Later tin was lithographed with details or painted. Very collectable are the many wind-up and battery-operated mechanical Santas. By looking inside many Japanese mechanical Santas, you will find their bodies constructed of tin cans from America – early recycling.

Chenille "pipe-cleaner" Christmas men found their way to the marketplace in the 1930s. Their bodies were basically chenille-covered wire twisted into a stick figure form. The colours they came in were red, white, green, or gold and they had either painted composition or printed paper faces.

Paper was the medium of choice from the earliest days of the production of Santas. In the mid-1800s improvements in printing meant brightly coloured, finely detailed pictures could be produced, and ornaments were then made from Father Christmas

ABOVE
German chromolithograph Father Christmas (1890 to 1910) in a long green jacket standing in the Man in the Moon – an image which often appears in Christmas ornaments.

RIGHT
German chromolithograph Father Christmas head with tinsel wiring. The blue colour was as common as red at the turn of the century.

ABOVE
American "Roly Poly" Santa produced by Schoenhut. Marked on the base: "Schoenhut Roly Poly, Patented Dec. 18, 1908".

RIGHT
A selection of hard plastic Santas manufactured in the United States in the 1950s and 1960s. The large Santa in back lights up. The other Santas held lollipops in their packs or sleigh, or were sold as toys. The Santa with the pack at his feet is also a bank.

BELOW
Tissue paper Père Noël *tree ornament with a paper face and mica-covered cardboard pack full of toys. Stamped on the back: "Made in France". (c. 1930).*

RIGHT
Homemade American Santas. The Santa on the left has a straw-stuffed body, cotton suit, tissue paper boots, cotton beard and a painted "walnut" face (1930s). The other Santa has a soft cotton-stuffed body, stitched facial features and a "curly" beard (1930s).

die-cuts. Santas have continued to be printed on a variety of papers and cardboard.

Technology developed in World War II gave the world plastic and the Santa market was forever altered. The new material was easily moulded and coloured; consequently, any pose was now possible and could be mass-produced. These plastic Santas portray the accepted Santa image of a rotund adult in a red suit.

Santa dolls are very popular with both doll and Santa collectors. They have cloth, cotton-stuffed bodies and buckram painted faces, or they have composition bodies and faces with lifelike features. They range in size from 30 to 90cm (12–36in) with cloth coats and boots. The advent of plastic created a moulded, plastic-faced doll with a red plush jacket, trousers and hat.

Not every family had extra money at Christmas to buy Santa dolls and figures. Homemade Santas are one-of-a-kind creations. For instance, someone lovingly made a St Nick with a straw-stuffed body, cloth suit, tissue paper boots and a painted walnut face. This character inherited a worm hole on his cheek that only adds to his appeal. Nature also provided pine cones, corn husks and dried apples for homemade Santa construction.

The collecting of Santas enjoys great popularity. Almost every family saved at least one special figure and even if it is now gone, its memory, imprinted in the child, is retained by the adult. This is the motivating factor for the beginning of many collections.

CHAPTER THREE

Transporting Santa

The only limit on Santa's travel has been the world's imagination. As the Santa legend developed, the way he moved around the globe broadened; in fact, a history of transport could be written by viewing his changing mode of travel.

Since St Nicholas is the first noted gift-giver, it naturally follows that the way he travelled would be immortalized by the St Nicholas figures. Early legend has St. Nicholas riding a white horse. As St Nicholas moved into Northern Europe, his story became mingled with pagan traditions and he was seen riding in a cart drawn by a goat.

THE SLEIGH

Northern cultures contributed the sleigh pulled by a reindeer to the legend. Consequently, when German manufacturers began producing Christmas items, they focused on the sleigh. Their choices of raw materials for the sleighs were very creative, utilizing moss, wood, iron, or paper. The reindeer had composition bodies either painted or covered with cloth or hide. Frequently the legs

LEFT
German chromolithograph illustrating a Santa driving a horse-drawn sleigh (1890 – 1910).

RIGHT
Japanese Santas, sleighs and reindeer. The composition Santa on the right, wearing a red flannel coat, is sitting in a cardboard sleigh pulled by a composition reindeer (1920 – 1930). The cotton batting Santa on the left is sitting in a cardboard sweet container sleigh pulled by a cotton batting deer (1930s).

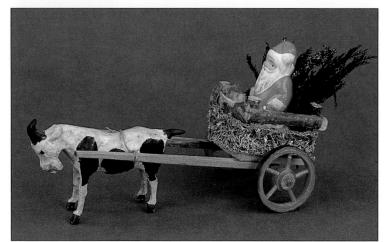

ABOVE
German composition Santa with a purple flannel coat and an unusual grey beard driving a wooden sledge filled with toys (1910).

RIGHT
German composition Santa in a moss cart pulled by a composition goat (1910 – 1920).

LEFT
This group of Santa sleigh sets from the 1920s and 1930s shows the wide variety of styles created.

were carved wood and antlers were fabricated with metal. The sleigh driver had a German composition body and rabbit-fur beard.

From early times to the present the sleigh has remained the method of transport visualized when thinking of Santa Claus and sleighs through the decades have been produced from a myriad of materials. The early sleighs were pulled by one reindeer, but seven were added by Clement Moore in his poem, *A Visit from St. Nicholas*. Any number of a variety of antlered animals can be found at the head of the sleigh.

The celluloid sleigh and reindeer appeared in the marketplace around the 1920s and stayed popular until celluloid production

was closed by World War II. These sets range in length from a tiny 2cm (1in) Santa, sleigh and single deer to a 60cm (2ft) ensemble with eight antlered reindeer. The sets can be mounted on a board, moulded as one piece, or assembled from individual pieces.

Sleigh and deer groupings were also assembled using a variety of materials – celluloid deer pull a cardboard sleigh driven by a composition Santa. "Marriages" were sold, but more often families assembled them from individual pieces. After World War II plastic sleigh sets flooded stores and are still popular today.

Motion is part of the Santa and sleigh scene. There are in existence some rare iron pull toys. Mechanization of the sleigh

RUDOLPH, THE NINTH REINDEER

An example of a contemporary concept becoming firmly entrenched in the Santa legend is Rudolph the Red-Nosed Reindeer. This story of a reindeer who was different and rose to fame guiding Santa's sleigh on a foggy Christmas Eve was created as a giveaway pamphlet by the Montgomery Ward Company in 1939.

As a result of the story's great popularity, it was developed into a song in 1947. The story and song, as well as figures of Rudolph, are a fixture of every Christmas season.

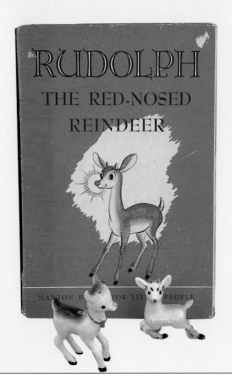

RIGHT
Rudolph the Red Nosed Reindeer *story book, hard plastic tree ornament and badge (1940s – 1950s).*

ABOVE
Hard plastic Santa sets (1950s to 1960s). The Santa on the left is a pull toy on wheels. The Santa on the right is standing in a cart – a variation of the sleigh theme.

RIGHT
An American 1950s hard plastic 30cm (12in) Santa riding a reindeer.

LEFT
*Biker Santas (1950 –
1960). (Left to right)
Japanese wind-up metal
bike with a celluloid
rider. American hard
plastic figure. Japanese
wind-up metal bike, with
soft plastic Santa and a
celluloid balloon.*

MODERN TRANSPORT

includes friction, clockwork, wind-up and battery-operated toys. Tiring of the sleigh as a method of transport, Santa has sometimes turned to other means of winter locomotion. He has elected to ride horses, goats and deer. He adopted skis when skiing gained popularity in the 1920s and for variety turned to sled riding and ice skating.

Wheels continue to be of interest to Santa. He has been seen riding tricycles, bicycles and motorcycles. As trains became a major method of transport, Santa kept up with the times by playing engine driver, passenger and brakeman. He also starred in train stories.

As motorized vehicles replaced animals as the transport of choice, Santa kept up with the modern trends and traded in his deer for a car. Santa prides himself on operating everything from the horseless carriage through trucks to the latest models in sports cars.

Santa has not, of course, neglected travel by water. He is an expert at paddling a canoe and is also skilled at operating a speedboat. He has ridden in tugboats, ferryboats and steamships, among others.

When the world turned to the skies for travel, Santa was already there – but in his sleigh. Having experienced travelling on

RIGHT

Santa skis! The Japanese composition skier on the left is on pressed cardboard skis with wooden poles (1930s). The American hard plastic Santa on the right uses metal skis (1950s).

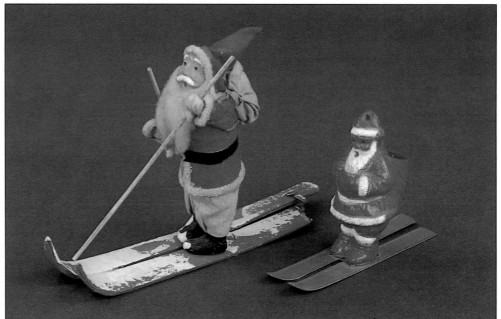

ABOVE

Santa's train is a Japanese mica-covered cardboard sweet container with a composition Santa head (1930).

RIGHT

Santa updates his flying machine! Japanese cotton batting Santas in cardboard aeroplanes, (c. 1930).

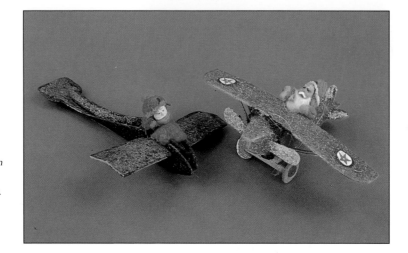

ABOVE

A Japanese cotton batting Santa piloting a celluloid canoe (1930s).

SANTA KEEPS BUSY

Santa has skills and talents that extend beyond the world of transport. Of course much of his time is spent keeping track of children's behaviour and creating holiday toys.

Advertisers and illustrators have always been quick to combine Santa Claus with new inventions. It was not uncommon to see Santa paired with the telegraph and the telephone. Currently, he can be seen on television using a copier, computer and fax machine. The public is led to believe that the North Pole is packed with the latest in audio-visual equipment.

Based on his appearance, it is obvious that Santa enjoys a good meal. This fact has pointed the way for advertisers to enlist him partaking of everything from alcohol and cigarettes, to soft drinks and sandwiches to biscuits and sweets. Will the present trends in health and fitness not only change how he is used by advertisers, but also alter Santa's physique?

Holidays also happen to Santa. The world has observed him on the covers of magazines sunning on a beach and enjoying tropical climes. Advertisers and greetings card illustrators have also portrayed him fly-fishing, playing tennis and relaxing on a cruise ship.

stars and with the moon, he soon adapted to travel by hot-air balloon and lighter-than-air Zeppelin or airship. Aeroplanes were his next challenge and he became so adept he advanced to jets and then spaceships.

Representations of Santa Claus have reflected contemporary transport and used current materials and production techniques. The Santa legend never dismisses a source of transport when a new one is introduced. Consequently, children today still read about Santa riding a deer, driving a sleigh, or flying Concorde; and figures are still being made that show him engaged in all activities from the earliest carts to current model cars.

RIGHT
Santa planning his delivery route.

CHAPTER FOUR

The Christmas Tree

HISTORY

bscured by the mists of time, the origin of the Christmas tree will never be known. However, every culture throughout history has used evergreens for celebration and decoration. The known origins of Christmas as a holiday – Saturnalia, Winter Solstice and Yule – all enshrined evergreens, and the green ritual migrated with these holidays as they moved to shape Christmas.

The earliest written references to a Christmas evergreen occur in the 16th century. Phillip Snyder records in *The Christmas Tree Book* that on Christmas Eve in Latvia and Estonia, members of guilds escorted an evergreen tree decorated with roses to a celebration in the town square and in Alsace, Germany, ordinances limiting the size and the taking of evergreens for the Christmas celebration were in effect by the early 1500s. These original Christmas trees were displayed without decoration, but financial records from 1597 show that money was spent on apples, coloured paper, biscuits and decorative cord for the decoration of the tree.

LEFT
Although this tree is far from "picture perfect", this young man still is proud to pose at its side.

ABOVE

These three children are justly proud of their tree; they have even donated two of their dolls to hang on the tree.

LEFT

A lavishly decorated room with garlands of greens and a gas chandelier festooned with ivy. The densely ornamented tree features popcorn, foil and glass bead roping. Ornaments include wax angels, wire and paper baskets, many different glass shapes, glass beads and scrap. The wooden tree stand is surrounded by a Christmas garden with a variety of figures on a moss base enclosed by a folded wooden fence.

RIGHT
*A fully decorated tree
with a variety of
commercial ornaments
from Germany with
homemade cotton
embellishments.*

The Christmas tree folklore credited with popularizing the custom says that Martin Luther was inspired by observing stars shining among fir trees to use a lighted Christmas tree to emphasize to his children the holy season.

The connections between the German and British royal families is a popular explanation for the rapid spread of the custom of decorating a tree at Christmastime. In 1848 an engraving in the *Illustrated London News* portrayed Queen Victoria, Prince Albert, and their children around a Christmas tree decorated with sugared ornaments and candles.

German immigrants took the concept of the Christmas tree to all parts of the world. Family celebrations among these ex-patriates focused around the tree and changed what was often a civic symbol to a private honoured position in the home. The Christmas pyramid, a wooden construction often holding evergreen boughs with shelves for displaying toys and decorations, was a possible forerunner which influenced the development of the Christmas tree. It was designed to be lit with candles and was often elaborately carved. The pyramid was used concurrently with the Christmas tree, and often a room was decorated with a lighted pyramid and an unlighted decorated evergreen tree.

From these early rituals and practices, the general practice of decorating an evergreen tree with fruit, baked goods, small gifts, and homemade decorations such as painted and coloured eggshells,

LEFT
A German goose feather tree with red composition berries (1900 – 1920).

RIGHT
German feather tree from between the wars decorated with both reproduction glass beaded decorations and original ornaments (the angel is made of tin plate and was supplied with the tree; the string of beads is from c. 1900). 75cm (2½ft) high.

paper flowers, and paper stars gradually developed. These trees were delightfully and dangerously illuminated by candles.

From the earliest use of evergreens in the Christmas celebration through to the 19th century, the tree could be any species or shape, depending on what was provided locally by Mother Nature. It could, in fact, be extremely ugly until it was lovingly decorated by its adopted family.

The increasing demand for evergreen Christmas trees meant that naturally grown trees were harvested and marketed in the cities. Early in the 20th century, the idea of raising Christmas trees on farms began. These commercially farmed trees standardized the classical pyramid shape and provided a thick, amply branched living room adornment.

RIGHT
A rare late 19th century ostrich feather tree with candleholders. 35cm (14in) high.

LEFT
1930s to 1950s adaptation of a bristle tree from the Addis Brush Company. These trees were designed as table decorations and were not themselves decorated, 105cm (3½ft) high.

As Christmas trees became universal, a need for artificial trees was perceived. There were and are many reasons why families decorated an artificial tree. Environmentally, any tree but a live tree has always been a popular concept. Another reason to use an artificial tree is availability – forests are not within everyone's reach. Cost also played a role in the family decision to use an artificial tree, but the strongest and most popular reasons for not using a live tree are ease and convenience. Once the tree has been purchased, it could be used year after year.

The first and most cherished artificial tree was the feather tree. This tree made an appearance at the end of the 1800s in Germany. German trees dominated the market, but by the early 20th century Japanese and American feather trees were available.

Feather trees were constructed by wrapping wire "branches" with dyed feather – commonly goose, but sometimes ostrich. The ends of the branches were ornamented with red composition berries or candleholders. These covered branches were inserted into a wooden trunk to create a pyramid form from a few centimetres (inches) to 2m (6ft) in height. The trunk of the tree was wrapped to hide the wires and then inserted into a wooden base. In later years trees were constructed with feathers dyed with other colours. Another kind of tree is constructed in the same way, but with finely cut coloured paper substituted for the feathers.

A homemade artificial tree that was popular at the turn of the century in America was a natural tree that was saved from year to year. Of course after its first Christmas the needles on a

TREE STANDS

After the tree was selected and brought into the home, a major problem was apparent – how to keep it upright. Probably the earliest Christmas tree stands were a wooden "X" nailed to the bottom of the trunk, or a bucket or crock filled with stones and water to hold the tree, and provide moisture. As the popularity of trees increased, the invention and manufacture of numerous ingenious methods for securing and watering the tree developed.

Cast-iron stands in differing styles were the pioneer tree stands on the market. The cast work was often ornate and embellished with handpainted or lithographed designs, and homemade adaptations were occasionally added. The stand was mounted on a hinged wooden box made to be filled with stones or scrap metal for weight.

Tin, with its ease of fabrication, has provided innumerable Christmas tree stands. These stands were often brightly decorated and contained a reservoir for watering the tree. Novelty variations include a wind-up mechanism for slowly turning the entire tree, a music box with seasonal music and wiring for coloured electric lights.

RIGHT
This tree is supported by a cast-iron stand.

LEFT

Late 1960s aluminum
tinsel tree, 60cm (2ft)
high.

FAR LEFT

Late 1960s early Swan
brand, aluminum tinsel
tree. 30cm (12in) high.

natural tree would drop. The cost-conscious family would store
the bare tree and bring it out the next Christmas, wrapping its
branches in white fluffy cotton before decorating it. In this fashion
one tree could be recycled for many years.

Plastic, "the miracle of the modern world", provided the
next generation of artificial trees and is still being used today.
Early plastic trees bore little resemblance to an evergreen tree.
They were solidly dark green without any variation and had long
stiff "needles". They could be disassembled and stored in a box,
but it was a common practice to store them fully decorated.

Current plastic trees show significant improvement, with a
variety of types representing many different species of trees. The
fabrication is lifelike, brown branches and trunk contrast with

flexible needles in various shades of green.

In the 1950s the aluminium Christmas tree appeared. Available
in a large number of sizes, it was a bright, sparkling holiday
adornment. For safety reasons strings of light could not be used
on its metal construction so illumination was provided by floodlights shining on the tree, sometimes enhanced by a revolving
series of coloured gels placed over the light which caused the tree
to shine with changing colour.

The Christmas tree survived another "craze" – the flocking
of live trees. This brief trend was so popular that it was featured
on the cover of magazines. The trees were flocked either profes-
sionally or with do-it-yourself kits available in colours ranging
from bright pink to blue, purple and white. Trees were either

1960s foil and glass tree from Germany. 25cm (10in) high.

Original aluminum "Silver Pine" tree, made in England c. 1960. 75cm (2½ft) high.

completely covered with the flocking material or lightly dusted as if with snow. The flocking process was not exclusive to live trees. Those seeking the convenience of an artificial model could purchase their plastic tree in all the latest flocked colours.

LEFT
A selection of soft metal ornaments (late 19th century). Their faceted edges are designed to reflect the lights on the tree.

ORNAMENTS

The earliest Christmas trees were displayed in their natural beauty, without ornament. The first known decorations were fruits, baked goods, nuts and paper flowers. Homemade trimmings advanced the ornamentation of the tree. Paper stars and silhouettes, coloured eggs and small toys and gifts all added to the beauty of the tree.

The practice of making homemade and edible ornaments remained standard through the 1860s. The confections became more ornate and foil, silvering and gilding increased the tree's lustre. By the 1870s manufactured decorations began replacing homemade ones.

During the period from 1870 to 1910, the largest assortment and the most finely crafted embellishments ever seen for the seasonal display became available. Cottage industries in Germany and other parts of Europe provided ornaments to the world.

Soft metal, cast in fancy geometric shapes and enhanced with lacquered colours and faceted and polished surfaces, was used during the 1870s. Wire, silvered or gilded, was bent into unbelievably elaborate forms from baskets to animals. Icicles were also fashioned from twisted metal, the perfect material to catch reflections of light.

Wax figures were realistic and perishable. The most popular

LEFT
*Chromolithograph angel
with a tissue paper skirt
(1890 – 1910).*

RIGHT
*Scrap angels with tinsel
and lametta (1890 –
1910).*

BELOW
*Scrap Father Christmas
mounted on cardboard
with a tinsel trim (1890
– 1910).*

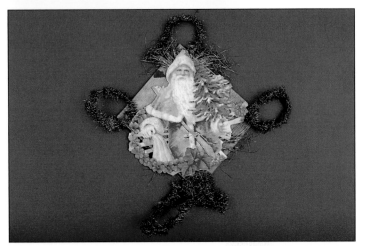

LEFT
Three hollow wax figures with mica decoration and metal ring hangers. 7.5cm (3in) high.

BELOW
Wax over composition angel. Painted facial features, spun glass wings and blue net skirt. 10cm (4in) long.

wax figures were angels, made by moulding a wax coating over a composition base from 5 to 25cm (2–10in) high. The features were delicately detailed with paint and finished with human hair, cloth or paper clothing, and cloth or foil wings. Wax figures were also produced by solid and hollow moulded processes.

Chromolithography and the "scrap" rage allowed the creation of ornaments limited only by the imagination of the maker. These colourful pictures enhanced by ribbon and tinsel increased the variety of tree ornaments. The relatively inexpensive "chromo" ranged in size from a few centimetres (inches) to complete figures 30cm (12in) or more long. Popular subjects included angels, children, Santa and winter scenes.

Dresden, Germany, gave its name to the most exquisite of all Christmas tree ornamentation. Fashioned of pressed "paperboard" embellished with gilding, foil, colours, wires and cotton, these flat or three-dimensional figures are extremely lifelike. They were created in every conceivable configuration – animals, edibles, furniture, transport. The labour intensive production process made Dresdens comparatively expensive, and this fact, plus their fragility, makes them rare and expensive today.

Cotton wool was used to make several types of Christmas trimmings. One style involves the formation through heat and pressure of a hard, solid figure. Commonly seen in this style are snowmen, people, fruits and vegetables. A second style of cotton

ornament involves forming the cotton fibre into fluffy sheets. This cotton batting was both shaped into three-dimensional figures and used to produce flat figures and clothing.

Cotton batting was frequently combined with chromolithograph paper and spun glass to create more detailed ornaments, and it was tucked into Dresden slippers or metal baskets.

Christmas tree ornamentation was revolutionized by the development of the blown-glass cottage industry in Europe, primarily Germany. The ancestors of today's glass ornaments were kugels from the German word, *kugeln,* meaning glass ball. Produced both in Germany and by German immigrant glass blowers in the US, these ornaments were primarily balls (2.5–30cm

RIGHT
German blown glass ornaments (1920 – 1940). (Top row, left to right) Yellow Santa – 5cm (2in); Santa with red lacquer – 5cm (2in). Second row, left to right) Snowman – 7.5cm (3in); Santa – 10cm (4in); silvered Santa – 7.5cm (3in); Snowman – 7.5cm (3in). (Bottom row, left to right) Clip-on unsilvered tree – 10cm (4in); Santa with red coat – 10cm (4in); silvered Santa – 10cm (4in); Santa – 10cm (4in); clip-on red tree – 10cm (4in).

BELOW
German blown glass ornaments (1920 – 1940). (Top row, left to right) Child sitting on a comet – 7.5cm (3in); child tied in a sack – 6cm (2½in); silvered clown with a green suit – 7.5cm (3in); child's head, silvered with flesh tone face and glass eyes – 6cm (2½in). (Centre) Devil's head – 11cm (4½in). (Bottom row, left to right) Girl costumed as clown – 10cm (4in); pipe with Queen's head bowl – 12.5cm (5in); clown – 5cm (2in); gold pear – 10cm (4in).

(1–12in) in diameter), but some were pears or bunches of grapes. Because of their thick glass walls, kugels are very heavy and durable, and they were frequently hung from ceiling beams and doorways.

The use of a gas flame instead of a wood fire by the glass blowers led to lighter and more sophisticated ornaments in a variety of shapes. Free-form and moulded glass, and the use of applied embellishments, reveal the craftsmanship and creativity of the workers. Once the glass was shaped, it was usually silvered on the interior, and the exterior was coloured with translucent lacquers, shiny opaque paints and frosted coatings.

These glass ornaments could be combined with other

RIGHT
German blown glass ornaments (1920 – 1940). A collection of silvered fish with various lacquered colours ranging in size from 5cm (2in) to 15cm (6in) high. The blue seashell on the left side is 3.5cm (1½in) high. In the upper right hand corner is a 7.5cm (3in) high blue beehive with painted silver bees (note the unusual cap). The insect world is also represented by two beetles and a moth.

BELOW
A group of unsilvered Victorian ornaments embellished with lametta wire, tinsel, scrap and Dresdens (Left to right) Musical instrument – 15cm (6in) high; basket – 7.5cm (3in) high; musical instrument – 12.5cm (5in) high; girl riding in a hot-air balloon – 12.5cm (5in) high; ship – 12.5cm (5in) high

materials. Tinsel or lametta wire was often wrapped around spheres or hot-air balloons. Pieces of chromolithograph scrap might be placed among the lametta or glued on the flat glass face of a snowman or Santa. Fabric flowers, composition berries and cotton batting were frequently used to make the finishing touches on glass ornaments. Moulded glass birds were perched on wire-spring legs which twisted into metal clips that snapped easily on to the tree. The birds had two basic types of tails, spun glass or feathers, and they sported spun glass wings if the ornament had a moulded indentation on each side. Metal clips were also attached to other glass ornaments such as Christmas trees, mushrooms, fruits and flowers, produced in many different shapes, sizes and

RIGHT
Examples of patriotically coloured ornaments produced for the American market (1920 to 1960).

RIGHT
Examples of patriotically coloured ornaments produced for the American market (1920 to 1960).

BELOW
Large coils of red and silver glass bead roping made in Japan. The small roping with unsilvered pink and blue beads was made in Germany (1920 – 1940).

colours. Glass beads were strung together into long strands that could be draped over the branches of the tree.

The period from World War I to World War II was a time of increased industrialization and mass production. Christmas ornaments followed this trend. Ornaments were sold in boxed matched sets. The market was flooded with sets of balls and simple shapes. Although speciality figures were still available, families usually purchased one "special" ornament every year. To capitalize on the nationalistic pride, ornaments of many styles were coloured red, white and blue both in Britain and the USA.

Countries other than Germany also began to produce Christmas ornaments and decorations. Sets of brightly coloured balls were produced in Poland.

An ornament that remains popular to this day was created in Czechoslovakia. Sections of wire were strung with small silvered and coloured glass beads and then formed into geometric shapes such as the outline of a house, church, star, and three-dimensional boxes. Occasionally, the central point of the ornament was a larger lametta-wrapped glass ball.

Japan was the next country to enter the glass ornament market. They utilized mass production and were able to ship large quantities of ornaments to the world. The detail was not as precise as the German cottage crafters, but the ornaments were brightly coloured and inexpensive.

Americans, anticipating the cessation of trade during World War I, had stockpiled German ornaments. When this supply was depleted, a domestic ornament industry came into being with the emphasis on mass production and boxed sets.

The disruption and destruction of World War II changed the Christmas tree. German production ceased entirely, and ornaments that were available were locally produced. In the US traditional materials were no longer available, but in an effort to maintain some production, clear glass ornaments with a few bands of coloured paint were manufactured. In Britain, many wartime ornaments were made by German prisoners of war.

After the war, consumer demand increased, and Germany again produced glass Christmas ornaments. These products can be found marked US Zone Germany, USSR Zone Germany and West Germany. As materials became available, glass ornaments were again silvered on the inside, and detailed and coloured on the exterior. An increase in textured, frosted and sanded surface details marks many figural ornaments.

In the post-war period raw materials were once again available for consumer use, and new materials developed during the war

RIGHT
Boxed sets of "Shiny Brite" ornaments made in the US (1950s).

BELOW
Glass beaded ornaments (1930s). All were made in Czechoslovakia except for the ornaments in the upper left-hand corner – cross and spoked sphere – which are Japanese.

RIGHT
China bell ornaments made in Japan.

ABOVE
Two boxes of lead icicles (1930s).

RIGHT
Hard plastic ornaments popular during the 1950s. The silver ornaments have a prism effect and the carousels contain propellers which sparkle when they turn, due to the heat of a light bulb.

LEFT
Uncommon paper ornament probably used to contain sweets or toys – German Man-In-The-Moon (1880s–1890s).

RIGHT
Three types of unsilvered glass ornaments produced in the United States during World War II when metals were scarce. (Note the paper cap on the bell.)

CAPS

were adapted for manufacturing. Ornaments were created from layers of brightly coloured foil in unusual shapes that were stapled in the centre and then folded out for a three-dimensional look. Plastic replaced celluloid, and a huge variety of decorations developed. This 1950s plastic can be identified by its hard, shiny surface.

Hard plastic was the perfect material for icicles. The plastic could be readily moulded in twisted shapes to reflect the light, and sets were soon available in clear, white, or glow-in-the-dark.

Rapidly changing fashion affected the Christmas tree in this period. Theme trees, decorated with a single colour or a particular ornament such as blue glass balls were the rage in the US.

As with Christmas customs in general, little is discarded. Ornaments from every period mingle on the family tree. Styles from the past continue to be used, and Christmas trees can be seen decorated with fruit and baked goods, paper flowers, all blue ornaments, or all homemade. The 1980s and 1990s has seen the resurgence of interest in ornaments and decorations of the past.

Ornament caps or tops are a practical but interesting necessity. The neck of the blown glass ornament was clipped to accommodate the early caps, which were metal with a piece of wire forming two loops. The first loop of wire twisted above the metal cap and connected the ornament to the tree. The second loop was underneath the cap and wrapped around a piece of wood. The wood was angled through the hole in the top of the ornament and served as an anchor when the ornament was hung on the tree. Some metal caps were glued directly to the ornament. At the turn of the century a metal cap and spring wire similar to the modern cap arrived, and the neck of the ornament was left intact for the spring cap.

Ingenious manufacturers developed paper caps that were glued on the stem of the ornament during World War II, when metals were strictly for military use only!

SCRAPS AND SCRAPBOOKS

In the 19th century it was popular to decorate gingerbread and confectionery with paper mottoes and flowers. These papers were commercially printed in sheets and the baker could tear off the "scrap" he needed to decorate the cake.

Germany improved the colour lithography or chromolithography printing process of the scrap until the embossed pictures could be mass produced. The scraps were exported to England and the US where they were keenly collected and pasted in albums. Scraps were added to calling cards, lovingly made into greetings cards, and combined with other materials to make Christmas ornaments.

Although many firms in England printed scraps, a German immigrant, Raphael Tuck, emerged as the leader in printing in England and most of the world. In his branches in Paris, London, New York and Melbourne, he used the chromolithography process to publish books, greetings cards, postcards, stationery and paper dolls.

An American, Louis Prang, is credited with popularizing the scrap and greetings card due to his perfection of the chromolithography printing process in the 1870s.

The greatest production of scraps was from 1875 to 1900, and they usually were sentimental in style and incomparable in their beautiful colours.

LIGHTING

Originally the lights of Christmas were reserved for the Christmas pyramid and were not used on the tree, but as these two customs merged, lights moved to the tree. During the 1870s, Christmas trees were lit by candles attached to the tree in several different ways. The majority of candles were held in place by candle clips, basic metal spring clips with a candleholder attached. The clips themselves were often decorated with stamped and lacquered shapes and designs. But the clip was inherently unsteady, and many unfortunate Christmas fires occurred. The solution was either to light the tree briefly with the family bucket brigade standing by, or to secure the candle.

To steady the candle, a counterweight was added to the clip to help balance the weight. The counterweights were often very elaborate and rivalled the ornaments for attention. The lantern, a hanging glass-sided ornament with a candleholder in the base, was only moderately successful as the tree was still vulnerable to fire.

Gas lamps provided an established alternative to candles and lamps in the home, and it was only natural that experiments with gas also involved Christmas tree lighting. But in 1879 Thomas Edison secured the future safety of Christmas trees with the invention of the electric light.

Electric Christmas tree lights were first used in 1882 in New York City, but they were not commonly accepted for use in people's homes for several decades.

By the time electricity became widely used, manufacturers were ready with strings of lights for the tree. The early sets were wired in series. If a bulb burnt out or was loose in the socket, the entire string went dark. The owner's task was then to search over the tree until the offending bulb was found.

A depiction of the German tradition of the Chriskindl's messengers and gift-givers – in this case a Santa-like figure – carrying with them a "tree of light".

RIGHT
Candleholders (1880–1920). Both the holders have counterweights to hold the candle upright. The one on the left has a solid gold painted composition ball and the one on the right has a counterweight in lacquered soft metal. The clip holders in the centre are embossed in various shapes and were originally brightly lacquered.

BELOW
(Back row, left to right) Victorian metal basket – 8.5cm (3½in) high; Victorian lacquered metal birdcage with metal bird; Victorian metal and coloured glass lantern – 7.5cm (3in) high. (Front) Gold metal basket – 5cm (2in) high (1930s).

Gas Christmas Tree Lights,

from *The Christmas Tree Book.*

". . . Over the years many attempts were made to find safer ways of lighting a tree, the most extreme version being an iron tree made by an English firm. It was lit by gas and advertised as the 'Improved German Christmas Tree.' In 1859, at St. James Lutheran Church in New York City, an evergreen was lighted by nearly two hundred gas jets that had been carefully built into it. In the years that followed other trees were similarly lighted . . ."

BELOW
*Electric tree light sets in
original boxes (1930s).*

ABOVE
*German glass figural
light bulbs (1900 –
1910). (Left to right):
Father Christmas; cat
with mandolin; songbird;
monkey; and clown.*

BELOW
*Japanese milkglass
figural light bulbs. (Left
to right) Bell shape with
Santa faces; Japanese
lantern; Santa Claus;
Japanese lantern; and*

*Santa Claus (1930 –
1940).*

Bulbs for strings of lights have undergone many changes. Figural glass lights have been and still are produced in a number of countries. Early figural lights were blown clear glass with painted details; later bulbs were manufactured of milk glass and then painted. These figurals have remained so popular that even after they burn out, the bulbs are hung on strings as ornaments.

Bubble lights were developed in the 1950s. A candle-shaped glass tube filled with liquid was fastened over the bulb. The heat from the bulb caused the liquid to bubble.

The modern Christmas tree continues to be the centrepiece of both private and public celebration of Christ's birth. "Red, yellow, black, or white – all are beautiful."

CHAPTER FIVE

The Christmas Garden

An entertaining Christmas tradition has developed from two cultures. From Italy came the "presepio", a representation of the scene of Christ's birth, which reached a peak of development in the 18th century. The scene was usually set in a fanciful Roman ruin, with figures carved of wood and dressed in elaborate flowing clothing of great richness and detail. The display was populated with the Holy Family, domestic animals and representatives of the Biblical stories of the Nativity, and completed by large numbers of angels and cherubim, with the angels sumptuously and dramatically garbed. Country and urban settings built as adjuncts to the Nativity scene provided finely detailed glimpses of Italian life.

The second cultural root originated in Germany and Central Europe and reached its greatest development among a Protestant sect, the Moravians, in Pennsylvania. This custom, called Putz (derived from a Saxon word, *Putzen,* to decorate), involved the construction of elaborate, lifelike displays in miniature.

The scene centred on the Nativity with ancillary vignettes of shepherds and Magi. Extending from this core other displays

LEFT
Fully decorated Christmas tree with finely detailed garden at the base. This garden recreates a farm scene with buildings, animals and people. The traditional fence encloses the scene. Note particularly that, while the room is illuminated by gas, the garden contains electric lights with overhead wires.

included the animals, two by two, ascending a road to the ark and people of all nations travelling to visit the newborn child.

These Putz scenes increased in size each year until entire rooms or even several rooms were consumed. The foundation for these displays were stumps, roots and contorted branches. Mountains of earth and rock, fanciful caves and grottoes were constructed. Water was added, and considerable plumbing was sometimes necessary to arrange waterfalls, fountains and rivers. Moss collected from the woods provided a green foundation, and the picture was further enhanced by evergreen branches and bare trees. The human and animal populations of the garden were hand-carved wooden figures.

Advancing technology influenced these Christmas creations.

Miniature steam engines were used to power numerous activities: a circular saw could cut wood; bales of hay could be loaded. Designers developed techniques that allowed fish to swim, carriages to roll, and people to work and play.

Electricity opened new vistas for displays. Lighted houses and street lights were possible, and with the advance of the electric train, the Putz could include trestles, signal lights and clanging bells along with rapidly speeding trains.

Of course, not every family spent several months planning and preparing a Putz or Christmas Garden. It was more customary for one or two scenes to be displayed. Favourites were, in addition to the Nativity, an under-the-tree village or farm scene and a flock of sheep with their shepherds.

In the beginning the buildings and figures of the Garden were handcrafted and carved by the builders. As the custom became more popular, the German cottage industry produced hand-constructed wooden houses. Increasing demand encouraged mass production; cardboard houses became available. Houses representing a portion of a village were frequently combined on one section of cardboard. The houses had cutout windows with a coloured paper backing that gave the illusion of interior lights. Their printed designs represented various façades such as brick, stone, or stucco.

These tableaux were populated with people and animals carved of wood or moulded of metal. It became customary for these smaller scenes to be surrounded by a fence. Wooden fences of various styles were manufactured, and many home-constructed enclosures were used. In the 1800s fence sets of cast metal that were miniature versions of the cast-iron fences of Victorian homes were used. Fence sets were also available in tin, and hedges made of feather tree branches and compressed moss were sold.

GERMAN FLATS

The tin soldier has a world of its own. Passionately collected and used to stage the battles of history, these soldiers constitute a major world hobby.

One style of soldier is a one-dimensional detailed figure, which originated in Nuremberg. These precisely painted "people" are produced from moulds carved by master engravers and show a high degree of artistry in their postures and clothing.

Sets of these tin figures, not all soldiers, were produced portraying all periods of history. A wide variety of scenes were available, from the Indians of the great South American civilizations to Victorian ice skaters.

These civilian scenes are ideal for populating the Christmas Garden. Sets of skaters, Santa's elves and a snowman band are particularly appropriate.

RIGHT
A selection of German sheep and goats (1900 – 1930s).

BRITAINS

A backlash to the horrors of World War I and World War II pushed the makers of tin soldiers to produce non-military items, and a highly popular field is "Britains".

The English firm of William Britain began by designing and producing miniature farm animals and buildings. They proved so popular that the line of metal models was expanded to include the circus, vehicles and city and country buildings. They also provided a complete garden scene in metal, with all the people necessary to maintain the floral display.

"Britains" were produced in metal throughout the first half of the 20th century. In the 1960s many items were reproduced in plastic, and the collecting of "Britains" remains a popular hobby to this day.

By the early 1900s sets of German paper houses were being retailed. These buildings had cellophane windows and a hole in the bottom or back so a light bulb from a string of Christmas lights could be inserted. These white cardboard sets came in various sizes painted different colours, and dusted with mica to provide sparkling snow. Many stood on individual bases which were surrounded by a wall or fence and decorated with moss trees and figures of people or Santas.

As the Japanese Christmas industry developed, sets of paper houses were exported. These houses were brightly coloured with more lavish coats of mica or snow. Bisque or celluloid figures were added to the garden.

Animals, both domestic and wild, for toys and Putz gardens were produced in profusion. The earliest German examples had composition bodies with carved wooden legs and were covered in fleece, cloth, or hide. The development of celluloid made a wide

LEFT
Composition Nativity figures from Germany. The baby Jesus is constructed of wax and is in a composition manger (1900 – 1940).

RIGHT
German Kings and attendants (1900 – 1940).

range of very realistic additions to the Christmas scene available. Celluloid animals were produced in Germany, Japan, and the US. Sets of farm and circus animals were cast in metal and later in rubber and then plastic.

The "housing market" also kept abreast of changing technology. Lithographed and painted tin was used for barns and commercial blocks. Varieties of cardboard houses with multi-coloured lithographed surfaces were sold in sets such as "The Pretty Village". Sweet boxes were printed as houses, and after the children consumed the sweets, another village scene could be added to the under-the-tree display.

German nativity figures were manufactured in sets of varying sizes, complete with barns, palm trees and Roman soldiers. These figures were cast in composition or plastic. More flamboyant and ornate sets in the Italian style were often modelled in Japan. Current plastic sets and individual figures are mass produced.

The rise in popularity of the model train has provided a wealth of newer material for use in the Garden. Many styles and materials are used for the miniature cities and villages, and the figures, who represent differing eras, are engaged in activities from swimming to manufacturing. The model trees and coloured surface materials developed for train displays preclude the necessity for collecting moss and lichen.

A fascinating aspect of the Christmas Garden is the practice of including equipment, buildings and figures without regard to size or time period. Animals of all sizes can be found, and separate scenes in the same garden show stories from the Old and New Testaments of the Bible next to a vision of the American Wild West next to tigers and monkeys in the jungle.

CHAPTER SIX

Decorating the Home

 People in Europe have decorated their homes at Christmas for many centuries. Decorating the home for the Christmas holiday was popularized and perfected in the US in the Victorian decades.

GREENERY

The Victorians, who revelled in all aspects of ornamentation, draped their homes in evergreens at Christmas. Any available evergreen was pressed into service, but the standard Christmas evergreen, which could be found in nearly every Victorian home, was the mistletoe, a berry that was synonymous with romance. Holly was the other popular berried leaf, and branches were tucked everywhere from table arrangements to curtain tie-backs. It was not uncommon to see sprigs of holly caught in upswept hair or sported in a coat lapel.

The traditional evergreens – pines, firs and spruces – were often fashioned into long chains or garlands which were wrapped around doorways and railings, or draped in swags along the wall.

Ivy, laurel, rhododendron, yew and boxwood could also be spotted throughout the Victorian home. Every painting and wall mirror had green branches jutting from the top or base, and arrangements bedecked tables and mantels.

Dedicated to the belief that "more is better", the Victorians were inclined to decorate the decorations. Garlands and boughs were often highlighted with flowers, glass beading and coloured or gilded papers folded into various shapes.

By the 1860s, British magazines carried articles to help the homemaker with Christmas decorating. In the US in 1910 *McCall's* gave detailed instructions about accessorizing the dining table. Women were encouraged to construct "candy-box" houses from cardboard, cover them with crepe paper, embank them in fluffy cotton "snow", and place one at each setting. The centre of this table would feature a small feather tree bearing tiny packages and guarded by a composition Father Christmas, or the homemaker could build a sugar-cube chimney complete with a Santa.

Magazines of the 1930s continued to educate their readers on up-to-date holiday decorating trends. The Christmas 1930 issue of *Woman's World* in the US recommended spreading Christmas

BELOW
The American
Magazine, *December
1933. Issue No. 6, Vol.
CXVI. Martha Sawyers
cover illustration. 21 ×
30cm (8½ × 12in),
134 pages.*

RIGHT
Better Homes and
Gardens *magazine,
December 1935.
Seymour Snyder cover
illustration. 21 × 30cm
(8½ × 12in), 56
pages.*

BELOW
Homes and Gardens,
*December 1952.
Christmas issue, No. 6,
Vol. 34, Harry Hants
cover illustration. 22.5
× 27.5cm (9 × 11in),
132 pages.*

CHRISTMAS NUMBER, DECEMBER, 1910

LEFT
McCall's Magazine,
December 1910. Cover
illustration by Carter
House. 20 × 27.5cm
(8 × 11in), 100 pages.

RIGHT
Original boxes of mica
"snow" used in
Christmas scenes
throughout the home
(1930s).

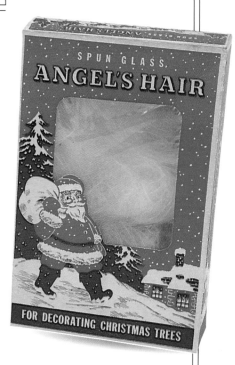

cheer with electric lights both inside and outside the home. Although public trees had been electrically illuminated for two decades, it was still not popular to use electric lights at home. *Woman's World* featured photographs with electric candles in windows and on mantelpieces. The outdoor pictures showed doorways lit with strings of coloured lamps and homes bathed in floodlights.

By 1934 electricity was accepted as part of the decorating ritual in the US. *Better Homes and Gardens* in their December issue promoted the use of a wreath and a lighted candle in the window and suggested that the homeowner use six- or ten-watt lamps in waterproof strings to outline the outside of the house.

The magazine also recommended using huckleberry branches in mantelpiece bouquets to serve as a backdrop for a Nativity arrangement. The *Better Homes and Garden* dining table centrepiece featured a small "live" spruce tree surrounded by toy figures.

TREES

The next major shift in festive decorations was in the 1950s. By this time magazines, still the purveyors of good taste, were telling readers how to decorate their Christmas trees. In 1955 *Collier's* hired six floral decorators to create different trees which were highlighted in the Christmas issue. The reader was shown trees trimmed in gold beads, foil and balls; or decorated on a "Victorian"

theme that featured sweets, nuts and bouquets of dried flowers. The other major discovery was the florist's foam ball, which could be covered with ribbon, sequins, or beads – anything that could be held down with a pin. Many trees in the 1950s were trimmed with hand-decorated florist's foam ornaments.

During this decade in the US communities united to create "block decorating". A city or town block would pick a theme and each house and lawn would be decorated accordingly. Many communities offered prizes to encourage originality. Families could then drive through various neighbourhoods to see the lights and lawn displays and compare them with their own.

FLOWERS

From the earliest times, flowers have been used as part of the celebration. Some of the earliest recorded trees were decorated with paper flowers. By Victorian times greenhouses and conservatories allowed the homeowner the luxury of real flowers in the dead of winter. Today, thanks to the development of hybrids, popular plants and flowers include poinsettias, cyclamen, Christmas cactus, and red and white carnations. Poinsettias, "ruler of the Christmas flowers", are available in most florists, street markets and supermarkets.

DISPLAYING A COLLECTION

Christmas collecting reaches a pinnacle as the holiday season arrives. After months of storage the treasures can finally be seen and used. All the new additions carefully collected over the year can be integrated with the prizes of past years.

If a large Putz, Crib or Christmas Garden is not appropriate to your home, many small scenes can be used throughout the

ABOVE
A child's china cupboard filled with celluloid and chalk Santas.

LEFT
Japanese bisque Santa Claus with his elves (1930s).

house instead; why not use table tops or shelves – any flat surface can become a spot of magic. On the bathroom vanitory unit a china sleigh filled with greenery and surrounded by "eight tiny reindeer" in celluloid could appear. On the opposite side could stand a bisque Santa Claus and a host of bisque elves, perhaps awaiting directions to load the sleigh.

Combining contemporary and antique decorative items can be most effective. For example, crystal fir trees, currently available, could form a background to blue, brown and silver blown-glass deer from the 1930s.

Toys make effective Garden scenes. A German wooden toy castle originally intended to protect instruments of war can be transformed into Santa's North Pole home. The addition of clouds

of Angel Hair and small white lights create a magical aura. The castle could be populated with a German tin-figure snowman band and Santa's elves from the 1930s and a tiny celluloid Santa and sleigh from Japan.

Do you have an open staircase? Leaning on the outside of the bannister rails on each step could be a different antique Christmas book with bright lithographed covers. If books are not right, a cardboard sleigh, Santa and reindeer could "mount to the roof-tops" going up the stairs.

When the Santa collection outgrows the mantelpiece, where do you turn? The authors group their Christmas Men by age. The oldest on the mantelpiece, the next on the front of shelves in the kitchen and the newest on shelves in the guest room.

RIGHT
A staircase ready for Christmas. Each step contains brightly lithographed "Twas the Night Before Christmas" books from 1886 to 1932. The table contains a crèche scene filled with antique German figures, animals and wax angels (1900–1940).

Original use can be ignored and the antiques displayed in new ways. Instead of using delicate glass icicles on the tree where they might not be seen, they can be suspended on fishing line from the dining room light to shimmer through holiday meals.

Many people are afraid to use fragile glass ornaments on the tree. They might fall or be pierced by the sharp evergreen needles. Feather trees provide an excellent solution. There are no sharp needles, and the wire branches provide secure places to attach the ornament hooks. The sparseness of the bare feather tree allows the delicate ornaments to be strategically placed so that each treasure can be clearly seen. A grove of feather trees, each displaying a different type of ornament, can be extremely effective.

A pile of fantastic Christmas postcards can be looked at and studied; could they be part of the decorations as well? One way to use these gems is to prop them against books on the bookshelves or against dishes in the china cupboard. In this way each one can be seen and the overall effect is festive and colourful.

Celluloid animals can be unsteady. If they fall down every time you use them in a display, try setting them on the branches of a feather tree until the tree is full. Then each animal can be seen and appreciated.

Kugels may be too heavy for the branches of an ordinary Christmas tree. Remember, in the "old days", they were often hung from beams or doorways. Just watch your head – the kugels are probably stronger.

Cycles of fad and fashion continue. What was once a rage will probably surface again as fashionable. For "new" ideas for holiday decorating, look to the past.

THE EVOLUTION
OF WINDOW DRESSING

One of the first Christmas window decorations was a lighted candle in a window. The candles were placed there to guide "special" travellers, who vary in different countries and cultures, from The Holy Couple, Mary and Joseph, to The Christmas Stranger, or The Christmas Visitor. In time, the reason was forgotten, but the candles had become part of the holiday.

Eventually the candles were electrified, allowing greenery to be used safely in the windows. Although various arrangements appeared in windows, the most enduring was the wreath made of evergreens and trimmed with pine cones, berries and ribbon. The first artificial wreaths were made of crepe paper, chenille or cellophane and for some reason were mostly red instead of green. They were trimmed with bells, glass balls, and ribbons. A cardboard ring wrapped in silver foil with foil bells and a red ribbon hanger was a homemade version of the wreath. Plastic wreaths came next, usually green with red plastic berries. They were easy to clean, but faded in the sun.

The electric candle appears alone or in groups and is available in every colour made by bulb manufacturers, but the most popular are still white, yellow, or red.

ABOVE
Window decorations have always been popular at Christmas. Shown on the left is a cellophane wreath with a cardboard electric candle and foil holly leaves. The small wreath is red chenille with erikamoos and fabric poinsettia trim

(1930s). The electric candle is cardboard in a lithograph metal candlestick (1920s).

RIGHT
Paper four-sided lantern that once housed a candle (1940).

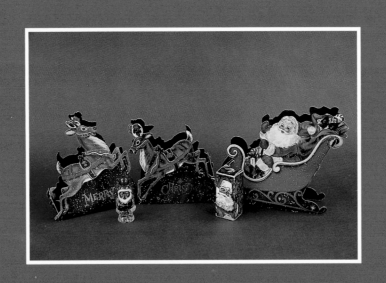

CHAPTER SEVEN

Christmas Shopping

D epending on your point of view, Christmas shopping is either wonderful or your worst nightmare. Realistically, your feelings are irrelevant, you have to shop for Christmas. There are only three possible ways to avoid the experience – cajole someone to do it for you, employ someone to do it for you, or refuse to do it and risk a lifelong association with Mr Dickens' Scrooge.

How did all this shopping stuff get started? Gift-giving at Christmas had been popular for several centuries when businessmen in the middle of the 19th century started to notice the commercial possibilities of the holiday.

Shopkeepers started embellishing their establishments with seasonal greenery and advertising "holiday specials". They discovered that promoting stock as "Christmas Presents" helped sell the merchandise. People's lives were starting to get busier, and the merchant's suggestions could be helpful timesavers.

The Victorians embraced the notion of Christmas shopping. Consequently, by the turn of the century, shopping was synonymous with Christmas in Europe and America. Despite this popu-

ABOVE
Celluloid and metal badges used to advertise department stores (1920–1960).

83

larity, many people found the process exhausting. In the December 1910 issue of an American magazine, the editor devoted a page to "Christmas Shopping". Some of the suggestions were:

★ Make up your mind that shopping is a real pleasure and not a burden.

★ Go about your shopping in a cheerful mood.

★ Begin just as early as you can.

The editor understood that cutting someone off a Christmas gift list might hurt a friend's feelings. So ideas were given for a workable solution. The final suggestions were:

★ Determine how much money you have to spend and spend that and no more.

★ Cut back on your list rather than run into debt.

SHOPPERS' BADGES

Shops realized that Christmas shopping was getting some negative publicity; they countered with holiday promotions. Badges suggesting "Shop at Klein's" were distributed to pedestrians along the street. Once the shoppers were lured into the store, they were given a badge that read, "I Shop at Klein's". These badges usually sported the happy smiling face of Santa Claus, subtly implying that he, too, shopped at Klein's.

The metal or celluloid badges sometimes gave specific directions – "Visit our Toyland" or "Meet me at –". Other badges were more general, simply stating "Merry Christmas" and giving the shop's name. Other businessmen who noticed the success of this campaign started to distribute badges promoting their product or their establishment. Finally, entire communities utilized the marketing technique with "Shop in (town name)" badges.

MAIL-ORDER AND ADVERTISING

The 20th century standardized mail-order shopping. Housewives who were too busy or lived too far away from major stores could do their shopping by mail. There would not be any crowds to push through or wait behind. The shopper could also resist the temptation of spending over their limit. Bellas Hess & Company of New York City ran a two-page advertisement in the 1907 December issue of *Pictorial Review* instructing readers to send in their money and item number today; if they were not satisfied, their money would be returned. The mail-order shopper was not

LEFT AND
BELOW
*Western Auto Associate
Stores' Christmas
catalogue, plus some
inside pages.*

RIGHT
Sheaffer's pen advertisement from The American Magazine *December 1933, which features the National Recovery Act logo.*

LEFT
A "Coca-Cola" advertisement from The American Magazine *December 1933 issue, encouraging the reader to "bounce back" with "Coca-Cola". The National Recovery Act logo appears at the bottom of the advertisement.*

completely free from sales pressure. A "Pure Silk Scarf, A Present Any Lady Will Appreciate" and "Dress Sweaters, Every Man Wants One Of These" were just some of the embellished offers.

Magazines noticed the success of their advertisers and a few developed mail-order businesses. A 1930 Christmas issue of *Woman's World* advertised the Sixth Mail Order Anniversary Specials and offered a virtual emporium of shopping treasures. The magazine encouraged its subscribers to "shop with your pen instead of your purse" and that year promoted dolls that "walk, talk and some of them sleep" and a Colonial jug lamp that was "reminiscent of Colonial days, yet highly modern". Other magazines avoided the mail-order business, but advertised a subscription to their magazine as the ideal Christmas present.

The depressed 1930s should logically have seen a slump in Christmas shopping. Although the activity of stores did decrease during the Depression, especially in the US, the holiday frenzy survived. Stores, manufacturers, and advertisers continued to promote spending money on Christmas gifts. A 1933 full-page Sheaffer's advertisement in *The American magazine* even appropriated the depression theme stating, "Proud gift! . . . at savings up to $4.75 – for the first 'recovery' Christmas". The advert also displayed the NRA symbol of Franklin Roosevelt's New Deal.

The 1930s found shoppers looking for "new gadgets" to give their families and friends. Prevalent selections included radios, typewriters, refrigerators, food mixers and cameras. Cars and car heaters also were promoted as Christmas presents.

LEFT
Examples of books distributed during the holidays in department stores. The books targeted both adult and child audiences (1930 – 1950).

BELOW
Greetings card announcing a subscription to the magazine The Farm Journal. *The editors utilized the Christmas gift idea to increase their readership (1920s).*

Magazines continued to help their readers shop for Christmas by running "Christmas Buying Guides." *Better Homes and Gardens* reviewed gifts for ages 8 to 18 in their December 1934 issue. The suggestions were divided into "boys" and "girls." The boys' gifts included American Indians and circus sets for the younger boys, and a telephone and telegraph signaller for boys aged 12 to 18. The girls' gifts ranged from doll sets to sewing and weaving machines.

The department-store Santa has been around in major cities since the turn of the century. However, it was not until the late 1930s and early 1940s in America that the idea became widespread. This kind of in-store promotion was an outstanding lure to shoppers and their children.

ABOVE
A 1929 celluloid calendar that was used for a holiday promotion.

LEFT
Woolson Spice Company's "trade card". Victorians enjoyed collecting these cards and mounting them in "scrap" books. The Santa on this card shows the transition from the stern-faced Father Christmas to the rotund Santa Claus.

RIGHT
An early 1900s felt pennant calendar used to create holiday goodwill among customers.

An entire advertising campaign was built around the store Santa. After the children told Santa what they wanted for Christmas, he would reach into his bag and pull out a gift. The "gift" was often a Christmas storybook or colouring book that had the name of the store printed prominently on the cover. In later years "Santa" distributed cellophane stockings filled with small toys and games. Of course, the stocking had the name of the store printed across the cuff. Many of these items featured Santa Claus and are sought by Santa collectors.

Giveaways were not only the domain of department stores. Pharmacies, hardware and jewellery shops, and many businessmen handed out a Christmas calendar, ruler, or plate. The giveaway always carried their business name and frequently an address or phone number. Although the majority of the public probably

SANTA'S ARRIVAL
IN TOWN OR LAMBS TO THE ...

nother day greatly anticipated by children and department-store owners was Santa's arrival. Over the years Santa has made his first appearance of the season in hot-air balloons, helicopters, parachutes, motorcycles, limousines, wagons and of course the traditional sleigh and reindeer.

He was frequently the grand finale of community Christmas parades, and his arrival signalled the official start of the holiday shopping season. Quite often the Santa in the parade was the local department-store Santa Claus, and the parade crowd would follow Santa right into the store. After all, once the children had spied Santa Claus, they immediately wanted to give him their official list.

Children basically understood that this was not the real Santa, but one of that busy man's many helpers. The children would wait in long lines for their turn on his lap. Sometimes the wait was bittersweet if the child either froze in silence or cried hysterically. These small snags did not bother the children still waiting in line, because their minds were focused intently on their one special moment with Santa Claus.

Sometimes the store had one more Christmas service to offer to parents: a photograph of their child chatting with Santa. The picture could be purchased for a small fee and immediately became a Christmas treasure in its own right.

A B O V E
This photo of Santa Claus with a little boy is typical of the photos parents could purchase after their child visited Santa (1940s).

LEFT
This trade card details The N. K. Fairbanks Company's promotion of their "Santa Claus Soap". They capitalized on the Santa name and the exchange of "gifts" for a predetermined number of soap wrappers. This card is reproduced regularly (1880 – 1900).

RIGHT
The Fairbanks Company also promoted a soap named "Fairbank's Fairy Soap" and they displayed it in stores at Christmas in this box (c. 1900).

shopped at these businesses throughout the year, they made a point of visiting the store at Christmas to pick up their customer presents, which are also naturals for holiday collectors.

The 1950s found Christmas shopping back in the news, as the cover story of the December 1952 *Homes and Gardens*, featuring an article by Virginia Graham on "Christmas Shopping". Her first observation was that men made more of a fuss about Christmas shopping than women made over having a baby. Her humorous view of the holiday fracas focused entirely on women carrying the burden of the Christmas buying.

DECORATING
THE DEPARTMENT STORES

Like any adult today, you will be able to describe what department stores looked like at Christmas during childhood: they were glorious. Mechanical displays depicted Santa in his workshop surrounded by busy elves, children decorating the Christmas tree, or the reindeer pawing the snow on a rooftop that looked very much like your own rooftop.

Every time you returned for another glimpse of the display, you noticed a wondrous new detail.

When your parents were finally able to drag you away, your disappointment immediately disappeared when you realized that the large train display on the next floor featured several trains pulled by a variety of engines charging through tunnels and over bridges. They chugged slowly by villages and towns and weaved through farms that reminded you of your grandparents' farm.

Your parents were grateful for your behaviour and proceeded to do the majority of their shopping while you were mesmerized by the marvellous miracle of mechanization.

Advertisers continued to pull out all the stops for the Christmas season which, by the 1950s, arrived at the end of November. Christmas themes were present in a variety of advertisements, some that seem peculiar by today's standards. Beer, wine, spirits and cigarettes were all promoted – frequently by the holiday's number one citizen, Santa Claus. Attempts to increase sales of telephones urged Americans to put a telephone in their bedroom, kitchen, or hobby room. Telephones were also advertised as the perfect gift for teenagers. Televisions and gramophones were very trendy presents in the 1950s in the US.

The major promotions of today's Christmas often focus around the computer. Not only is the computer touted as the optimal family gift, if the owners have a modem, they can even utilize the computer to do their shopping. Is this the Christmas buying future?

The world of Christmas shopping has not changed very dramatically over this century. The tips that *McCall's* gave the 1910 shopper are all very timely today. Men allegedly still hate to Christmas shop. Mail order remains a popular alternative to physically facing the crowds, and advertisers get as much mileage out of the holiday as they did at the turn of the century.

LEFT
This 1950s pressed cardboard Santa head was used as a display item in stores at Christmas – 60cm (24in) high.

CHAPTER EIGHT

Home For The Holidays

he "Home for the Holidays" theme has been celebrated in songs, movies and books. It is one of those ideas that we all want in our dreams. Consequently, many Christmas activities are centred around the home.

HOMEMADE IS BEST

Food has always played a predominant role at Christmas. Women at the turn of the century usually did not work outside the home, and a major part of most days was devoted to cooking and baking in addition to other housework of course.

One of the most elaborate creations was the Christmas legend, the Plum Pudding. This dessert originated in England, but the recipe travelled wherever English colonists settled. Because the directions were time-consuming and painstaking, many magazines of the early 20th century tried to simplify or modify the procedure.

The 1907 Christmas issue of *Pictorial Review* recommended using a square mould that was easier to handle and insisted that the pudding should be lit as it was being brought to the table.

ABOVE
A typical mould used for Christmas plum pudding (1930s).

THE WELL-TRAVELED RECIPE

1lb each of dark raisins, currants, candied citron
(lemon peel), and ground suet
2¾ cups flour
2⅓ cups sugar
1 tsp each of salt, allspice, and ginger
½ tsp cloves
5 eggs
2 tbsp grated lemon peel
½ cup each of brandy and sherry

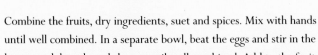

Arthur Albert Sharman emigrated to America in 1893. In an attempt to keep some familiarity in his new world, he carried with him many treasures from his English home.

Among these was a recipe for Plum Pudding that his mother, Keziah Cross Sharman, prepared every Christmas. When he married Annie Barrett in 1900, she prepared the Plum Pudding. As the family spread out across America, the pudding recipe followed. Descendants of Arthur Sharman have prepared this Plum Pudding every Christmas from 1900 till today.

Combine the fruits, dry ingredients, suet and spices. Mix with hands until well combined. In a separate bowl, beat the eggs and stir in the lemon peel, brandy and sherry until well combined. Add to the fruit mixture; stir well. Turn into a large well-greased mould with a tight-fitting cover. Place the mould on a trivet in a kettle or soup pot. Pour boiling water halfway up the side of the mould, cover the kettle and steam for four hours. Remove the mould to a rack, cool briefly. Invert on a serving plate, lift off mould. Serve at once, flaming, with hard sauce.

Tips: Grate the suet when frozen or ask the butcher to grind it. Heat the brandy prior to pouring over the pudding and light with a match to produce the flaming dessert.

LEFT
Two tins with Christmas scenes that were saved by families year after year and filled with holiday treats. The large box originally contained Nabisco crackers (1920 – 1940).

Their secret to successful torching was to heap lump sugar around the pudding mound and then add half a cup of brandy. The editor guaranteed a flaming pudding.

McCall's declared in their 1910 Christmas issue that plum pudding must be present on the table even if not one person took a bite and went on to describe several recipes that they felt sure would tempt even the fussiest appetite. *McCall's* felt that the only "orthodox" serving of the plum pudding was the ignited version. For teetotallers they also offered a "dry" recipe that did not include any brandy.

Busier complicated lifestyles dimmed the popularity of the plum pudding in the US. Women preferred grandiose decorated cakes that they could prepare in a fraction of the time spent on the pudding. But there were families who shared the same sentiment as *McCall's* – that it must be present every Christmas and so the tradition continues today. The pudding moulds are rather attractive and are sought by both kitchen and Christmas collectors.

Holiday baking included the preparation of a variety of biscuits, sweets and confections. Kitchens were stocked with exotic ingredients too costly to be kept in the larder. Many housewives channelled their baking skills into making Christmas gifts for friends or distant relatives that they could not afford to add to their Christmas shopping list, and "gifts from the kitchen" became another Christmas tradition.

LEFT
Inspiration *magazine,
December 1923.
Christmas issue Vol. 7,
No. 12. Alice Seipp cover
illustration. 22.5 ×
29cm (9 × 11½in), 16
pages.

Mothers recruited the entire family in the preparation of these gifts. Women shared only their best creations and constantly searched for "special delicacies" to add to their repertoire. Magazine editors recognized an opportunity, and it became difficult to pick up a Christmas issue that did not contain recipes for "edible gifts". The December 1923 issue of *Inspiration* recommended that housewives send their dainty biscuits and sweets to a friend who was a "business woman, so situated as not to be able to make them". The article listed recipes for coconut rings, pralines and stuffed dates, which all contained precious ingredients for cherished gifts. These dainties were often packed in tins that were either bought for the purpose, or appropriated from their original use as containers for commercial biscuits and crackers. They usually had decorative lids with a variety of scenes from old-world paintings to seasonal themes. These tins, especially those sporting Santa, are treasured by Christmas collectors.

Not every homemaker used a tin to contain their gifts. Some followed the advice of magazines like the 1930 Christmas issue of *Woman's World* that heralded homemade sweets as the only suitable gift for the person "away from home". They hinted that spending extra time creating your own packaging would further endear the gift to the faraway recipient.

Lily Haxworth Wallace, the "domestic science" editor of *Woman's World,* highlighted instructions for making a "confection doll" of figs, raisins, gumdrops, marshmallows and cocktail sticks. Children could be involved with the construction of the doll, and its decorative place at the table would cheer the entire family. The editor was dedicated to her readers and recommended that if they were doing any large-scale sweet-making, they should invest in a sugar thermometer and a marble slab.

Christmas cakes were an art in their own right. The decorative icings, trims and layers were testimonials to the dedication of the housewife. Hilda M. Whitlow in the December 1952 *Homes and Gardens* gave detailed recipes for exotic offerings for "Christmas Tea-Time". Her suggestions included Christmas Cake, Marzipan Petal Cake and Butter Cream Gateau. Their very names trigger an appetite whetted for holiday indulgence. Unfortunately, their beauty was often so overwhelming that people were reluctant to defile them with a knife.

This domestic version of the holiday produced many collectables. People search for Christmas recipes and cookbooks, and cherish those highlighted with "homey" illustrations and stories that give them a glimpse of the time. Biscuit cutters, rosette irons and sweet moulds with Christmas themes are so popular that they have generated their own branch of speciality collectors.

Tin biscuit cutters that had a special role in holiday baking. Biscuit cutters are very collectable today.

Families pass biscuit cutters down through the generations, and even the busiest family will try to produce at least one batch of biscuits with their treasured cutters. Other families elevate their biscuit cutters to a more regal position – as adornment for their Christmas tree.

The kitchen also produced the Christmas Dinner. Whether it was served on Christmas Eve or Christmas Day, the preparations were executed with the precision of military planning. The meal featured delicacies not offered at any other meal of the year. It was the one moment when the family was assembled in fellowship.

Authors such as Charles Dickens, Washington Irving and Louisa May Alcott immortalized the "Christmas Feast" for their fictional families, rich or poor. Homemakers realized the importance of this meal and devoted their talents to its success. Men had one time-honoured role in the Christmas Dinner – the carving of the fowl.

Traditions played an integral part in the Christmas meal. The best china, glassware, silver and linens were polished and pressed. If they were family heirlooms, they assumed even greater importance. A family that did not own "the best" of anything applied the same polishing and pressing to make "everyday" into the "best".

Other traditions developed around the Christmas dinner. Some families left one vacant chair for the "Christmas Visitor or Stranger". Other families always included a friend or family member who would otherwise have spent the holiday alone.

LEFT
These cardboard Santas were made from advertisements and strings. They were lovingly coloured with crayons by children (1920s).

Fortunate Christmas collectors who have family china, glassware and silver frequently search for pieces to complete, replace, or complement their heirlooms. If there are no family treasures, antique shops and department stores offer many opportunities to serve Christmas dinner beautifully.

HANDMADE WITH LOVE

Handmade gifts have been popular since the beginning of gift-giving, but became a necessity when money did not stretch to cover everyone on an ever-expanding Christmas list.

Once again, magazines came to the rescue with suggestions for handmade presents. Anne L. Gorman in 1910 stated in *McCall's*

that handmade gifts were more valued than shop-bought. She highly recommended needlework for a myriad of gifts from smoking pouches, handbags and handkerchiefs to pincushions and couch pillows. She felt that these pieces would be treasured, and that initials and a date should be present in the stitchery.

Another suggestion was to give handmade gifts to the "less fortunate", which gave the homemaker the opportunity to help someone without draining precious financial resources. In the December 1923 issue of *Inspiration,* ideas for this type of gift-giving are listed, but readers are assured that the idea would be appropriate for anyone on their list. Directions for rag dolls and woolly lambs made from cotton socks were the highlight of the article. Even in the prosperous 1950s, magazines were still endorsing handmade presents. The 1952 Christmas issue of *Homes and Gardens* gave directions for gifts that were "easy and inexpensive". These gifts were more sophisticated, with instructions ranging from a raffia lampshade or raffia slippers to make-up trays for travel. Old standbys such as work bags, stocking bags and dolls were still included.

Handmade Christmas gifts are not considered a collector's gold mine. However, quality needlework pieces always have a market value, and the addition of a Christmas date would certainly attract the obsessed Christmas collector.

GIFT WRAPS

Gifts cannot be discussed without mentioning gift wrapping, another activity that can be either a highlight or a nightmare of the holiday. Traditionally it has been approached in a positive light, with as much time devoted to gift wrapping as to purchasing the presents.

By the 1920s American stores offered gift wrapping as a standard Christmas service, but many people preferred the Christmas extra of boxing Christmas gift purchases. The shopper could then take the gift home and dress it in all the new wrappings and trims that were readily available. If the homemaker was creative, she could enlist her children's assistance and turn gift-wrapping into a family affair.

Magazines, realizing that not all of their subscribers were creative, dedicated space in their Christmas issues to some gift-wrapping ideas. Perhaps not coincidentally, there was often a form at the back of that issue enabling the homemaker to order the trims described in the article by mail.

Another Christmas tradition we have discovered is that some American families pass a box covered in worn, tattered wrapping from one generation to the next. It is carefully exchanged among family members year after year, thus carefully preserving the fragile, antique paper.

Many Christmas stickers, seals and gift tags have been accidentally preserved among tree decorations, or in more organized families they were intentionally saved. Their bright colours and

LEFT
Gift tags used to identify that special Christmas package (1920 to 1930). The dog in Santa's bag is a sticker from the early 1960s.

99

LEFT
Santa's Paint Book
published by Merrill Co.,
Chicago, 1949. This,
coupled with paints and
a brush, entertained
post-war children.

dated phrases create an interesting Christmas collage, and they are starting to attract serious attention among Christmas collectors.

CHRISTMAS FASHION

Entertaining in the home at Christmas demanded more from the homemaker than baking and cooking. She needed to wear the "right" dress and hairstyle. Once again she was able to turn to her magazines, this time for fashion advice. The December 1923 issue of *Inspiration* recognized that "Christmas time is dress-up time and a new dress is considered quite essential for the holiday festivities," and proposed that if you were over twenty-five, you should wear a conservative dress that would do for many occasions. The suggested colours were not the traditional Christmas ones, but coral, blue, or yellow in either taffeta or georgette.

Hairdressing was covered in the 1930 *Woman's World*. The author thought that hair should be styled according to the dress, especially if this was a "period" style. The magazine promoted "soft waves dressed close to the head or softly wrapping the hair in a knot at the nape of the neck", and cautioned against wearing a style that was "modern".

ACTIVITIES FOR THE CHILDREN

While all the aspects of Christmas in the home were important, it was the children that added lustre to the holiday. As the season approached, some children had difficulty controlling their behaviour. In many climates daylight hours were short and temperatures were low, which forced children indoors. They were torn between a strong desire to "be good for Santa" and a large amount of restrained energy.

Activities that kept the children occupied were the salvation of busy mothers during the holiday season. Manufacturers utilized the holiday themes, and stores sold an abundance of entertaining items that featured Santa, Christmas trees and winter sports. Over the last century, children have played with storybooks, blocks, colouring books, paint books, board games, playing cards and records that all have a Christmas theme.

These toys are an exciting area for Christmas collectors. They are also some of the most difficult to locate and afford. The early Santa board games are popular among Santa and toy collectors. Storybooks from the late 1800s often have lithographed Santa covers which also appeal to the Santa collector. There are people

(Left to right) Virginia Reel wooden jigsaw puzzle, 8 December, 1928 using the Norman Rockwell cover illustration from the **Saturday Evening Post.** *23 × 25cm (9¾ × 10½in); Santa Claus jigsaw puzzle using* **Ladies' Home Journal** *magazine cover. 22.5 × 30cm (9 × 12in); games advertised in the Jim Brown discount Christmas catalogue.*

A set of German wooden puzzle blocks (1890 – 1910). The detailed lithography allows six different pictures to appear as the blocks are rearranged. The set is kept in a paper-covered wooden box. The puzzle occupied Victorian children as they waited for Santa's arrival. (From the collection of Mr and Mrs James Boyer.)

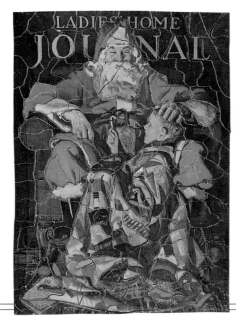

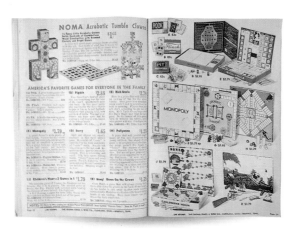

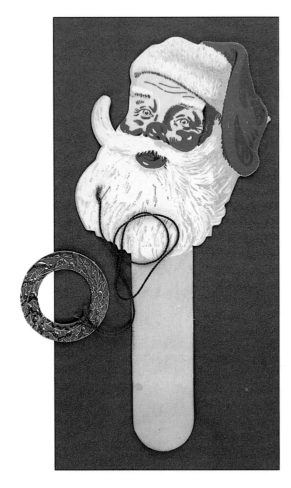

ABOVE

*78 rpm records (1950s)
that entertained children
with holiday music. To
attract the holiday
shopper even the record
itself shows a Christmas
theme.*

ABOVE

*Even the common ring-
toss game was recast for
the holiday season. This
cardboard version was a
bank giveaway from the
1940s.*

who collect only *Night Before Christmas* books. Puzzles, games and storybooks from the 1950s are still available and affordable, but they shoot up in value when the Christmas theme is connected with a popular cartoon figure. While the 1950s items are still obtainable, they will soon be the next endangered era of Christmas collectables.

Composing Santa letters was one of a child's favourite Christmas chores, especially if the family did not live near a community or department store Santa. Some children would work painstakingly for weeks; others would scribble furiously for several minutes. How the letter actually arrived at the North Pole was a custom that differed from area to area. A child might simply "mail" the letter to Santa; another might toss the letter into the fireplace so the smoke would carry it to the North Pole.

Many families have always had a family member, friend, or neighbour who dressed as Santa Claus and visited the children. He usually enquired about their behaviour and left a small present or treat. The Santa costume could be purchased or handmade. There were even Santa masks with beards. The masks were made of papier-mâché, cloth, or rubber, and the beard was usually composed of cotton batting. These costumes and masks provide another sideline opportunity for collectors. They surface in boxes of Halloween costumes and trunks of old clothing.

On Christmas Eve children were encouraged to leave a snack such as biscuits and milk for Santa Claus. The reindeer were remembered with carrots. These offerings were usually accompanied by a note reaffirming that the children had been very good this year. The next morning, the children would race to the tree and discover an empty glass, some biscuit crumbs, carrot tops and a "thank you" note from Santa Claus.

Advertisers soon picked up on the idea; a 1907 Ivory Soap advertisement features a little girl leaving a bar of Ivory Soap for Santa to use to clean off the chimney soot. Coca-Cola has for decades pictured Santa Claus by the tree enjoying a refreshing Coke left by thoughtful children.

There are many traditions in our homes at Christmas. Entire families combine efforts to meet holiday needs and deadlines. People who cannot be at home for Christmas congregate and prepare elaborate Christmas dinners that create their own special memories. Magazines continue to help us with holiday hints for baking, cooking, entertaining, dressing and gift wrapping. These Christmas issues will no doubt be collected by future generations to discover how we celebrated Christmas in our homes.

ABOVE
This buckram cloth Santa face mask has a cotton batting beard and an attached cap. This costume was used to delight children of all ages in the 1920s and 1930s.

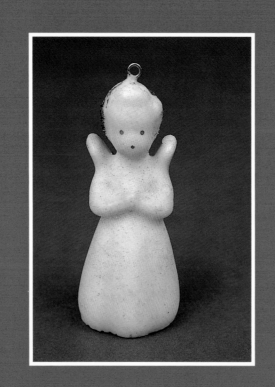

CHAPTER NINE

Christmas Spirit

Charity is very closely associated with Christmas. Media news teams feature Christmas stories about people's generosity and the broadcasts trigger more giving. Holiday benevolence has been popular since the second half of the 19th century.

Christmas charity has traditionally been handled in two very different ways. Some organizations and private individuals prefer the personal touch in their holiday giving. These people collect food and prepare baskets or boxes and deliver them to less fortunate families or individuals in the area.

Other contributors prefer to remain anonymous. They give or mail a monetary donation to organizations that solicit assistance particularly at Christmas and handle the distribution of food, money and toys.

In past decades children were also encouraged to help "poor children". Churches and schools had small banks which children were persuaded to fill with their pocket money, and as Christmas approached, a group of children would deliver the total sum to a worthy organization.

RIGHT
Children's Christmas carol song book (1940s). These books are often sought by collectors for their appealing holiday pictures.

Then there were the parents who wanted their children to know the "true spirit of sharing". These children were encouraged to go to their toy boxes and part with one of their special toys. For every child who dutifully selected a "favourite". there was always one who would try to convince its parents that a broken doll or truck was indeed the most favoured toy. But the parents always saw through these attempts and prodded until the best toy was dutifully packed for distribution.

The American Salvation Army is probably the most visible modern Christmas charity. Their Sidewalk Santas, bells, bands and collecting tins are synonymous with the holiday. In these days of increasing numbers of homeless people, organizations like the Salvation Army work ever more diligently.

The "sick and hospitalized" have also received attention at Christmas. Organizations such as the Red Cross and the National Tuberculosis Association mounted massive Christmas campaigns

LEFT
Celluloid and metal badges from the National Tuberculosis Association (1930 – 1950). The badges were part of a Christmas campaign to raise funds to fight TB. The badges commonly used the slogan "Health For All" or "Health To All".

ABOVE
The American Red Cross commissioned this poster from Harrison Fisher in 1918. This heroic pose inspired patriotism which, combined with the Christmas appeal, attracted blood donors.

to alert the public of the constant need. The Red Cross distributed posters and pamphlets encouraging people to give blood. The National Tuberculosis Association gave out badges and Christmas Seals in return for a donation. These solicitation symbols are very popular among Christmas collectors. They usually feature Santa Claus, and the Red Cross posters were frequently signed by famous illustrators such as Harrison Fisher and Dan Smith.

Christmas spirit was always evident at both churches and schools. Between the two, very few children were not recipients of community generosity. Many churches and schools gave sweets to children at Christmas. While the sweets was always appreciated, it was frequently the sweet box that received the majority of the child's attention.

Early American boxes were created in sepia tones featuring illustrations of winter scenes. They had a locking flap that opened at either end of the box and could be carried by a "shoestring" handle. Later, the boxes became more brightly coloured, being illustrated with pictures of snowmen or Father Christmas or Santa Claus. The box retained the original construction and handle through several decades.

Many children quickly ate all the sweets, while some savoured the sweets throughout the entire holiday period and others shared their wealth with the less fortunate adults. These sweet boxes are cherished among collectors, and it is not unusual to see a small private smile spread across the face of an aficionado who spies a Christmas sweet box.

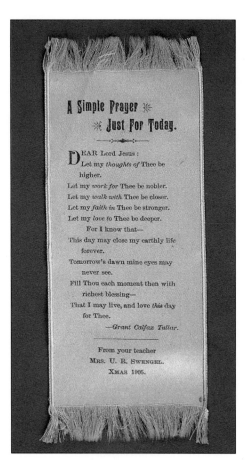

A Simple Prayer ✻
✻ Just For Today.

DEAR Lord Jesus :
     Let my *thoughts of* Thee be
          higher.
Let my *work for* Thee be nobler.
Let my *walk with* Thee be closer.
Let my *faith in* Thee be stronger.
Let my *love to* Thee be deeper.
          For I know that—
This day may close my earthly life
          forever.
Tomorrow's dawn mine eyes may
          never see.
Fill Thou each moment then with
          richest blessing—
That I may live, and love *this* day
          for Thee.

               —*Grant Colfax Tullar.*

          From your teacher
          MRS. U. R. SWENGEL.
               XMAS 1905.

ABOVE
*This silk bookmark was a
special Christmas gift
from a "Mrs Swengel" to
her students in 1905.*

Wishing you a Very Happy Christmas.

ABOVE
*A Victorian flat card that
highlights a common
theme – a household pet.*

Christmas plays or pageants were presented in churches, schools and private homes. Since the late 1800s booklets with Christmas poems and plays were available. Children would be assigned a poem or reading, or a part in the pageant. Those who played an instrument might be assigned a Christmas solo. Parents and relatives would proudly pack the church or community hall to listen to their children.

The programmes always had the most serious intentions, but audiences often had difficulty restraining their giggles when an angel lost her wings or a shepherd made faces at the audience.

These programmes were wonderful opportunities for children to exercise their dramatic talents and show off their feats of memory. The evening often ended with biscuits and treats and perhaps a visit from old St Nick. The booklets and programmes from these events are collectable, if only for a glimpse of a very special evening.

This fold-out Victorian Christmas card was made by Raphael Tuck and Sons, London.

Another popular Victorian Christmas card theme – children. The border of this flat card is made of paper lace.

CHRISTMAS CARDS

One of the most usual ways of expressing Christmas spirit is by exchanging Christmas cards. The practice of sending Christmas cards grew out of the Victorian use of decorated calling cards and of printed note paper and envelopes for New Year's greetings.

The card business was really made possible by the advent of the postage stamp and "Penny Post" in England in 1840. Prior to this innovation, postage was based on mileage and paid by the recipient when mail was delivered. Now the sender could bear the postage with a flat rate.

The first commercially printed Christmas card is attributed to Sir Henry Cole, the first Director of London's Victoria and Albert Museum. This card, designed by John C. Horsley and available in 1843, was sold from the shop "Home Treasury" owned by Henry Cole.

ABOVE
*A Victorian card with a
religious message.*

RIGHT
*An early 1900s
Christmas postcard with
the unusual depiction of
an African-American
family Christmas.*

ABOVE LEFT
*Turn-of-the-century
Father Christmas and an
angel inspecting a gift
list. This postcard was
mailed to a child with
instructions to be
"good".*

ABOVE
*This Father Christmas is
flanked by a candlelit
tree on this postcard
(1908).*

ABOVE
The difference between the Victorian cards and the Christmas cards of the 1920s is very obvious. Notice particularly the bright colours.

RIGHT
This card had both political and patriotic overtones for the family who received it (1940s).

The card, 8 × 13cm (3 × 5in), was a scene of a family enjoying Christmas dinner with side vignettes showing feeding and clothing the poor. The greeting read "A Merry Christmas and a Happy New Year To You".

By the 1850s improved printing techniques allowed the expansion of the card business. Now cards could be inexpensively multicoloured. Adopting the styles of the day, they could be trimmed with a wide variety of cut and embossed papers.

Prominent early printers of Christmas cards are Mansell, Goodall, Marcus Ward and Nister in England, R. H. Pease in America, Bernhard Ollendorff in Berlin and in Munich the

BELOW

A contemporary example of the holiday craze is this dollar bill with a matching Santa image glued on the front. A portion of the purchase price was donated to the Salvation Army.

RIGHT

Everyone develops the Christmas spirit – banks used Santa's image on the cover of their Christmas Club passbooks, matchbook covers and matches (1920 – 1940). Even

Western Union had a holiday heading for their telegrams in 1946.

Obpacher Brothers and Lothar Meggendorfer. These publishers hired artists to create their cards and held competitions for the best designs.

Throughout their 150-year history, Christmas cards have been a mirror of the styles and tastes of the times. Popular early pictures were of animals and children. An early fad was birds dressed and acting like people to bring the Christmas message.

As Victorian style gave way to the Art Nouveau movement, the appearance of Christmas cards changed also. An emphasis on nature, stylized natural lines, and muted colours marked this period.

Every subject of which man has knowledge has appeared on cards. Sometimes the emphasis is on family; at other times, country scenes, flowers, or winter have predominated. Particularly collectable are pop-up cards, large-format embossed nativity scenes, and anything by the highly popular artist Kate Greenaway. Collections by topic also hold great interest.

CHRISTMAS COMMUNICATION

Christmas telegrams were in fashion from 1930 to the 1950s. These holiday messages featured colourful Christmas pictures at the top of the telegraph blank. Those that show Santa are a welcome addition to a Santa Claus display.

Telephones made Christmas communication easier and more personal. The Bell System (AT&T), in a 1934 advertisement in *Better Homes and Gardens,* suggested "Share your Holiday Happiness by Telephone". They listed their rates after 8:30 p.m. as 35¢ for 75 miles and 75¢ for 275 miles.

CHRISTMAS SPIRITS, THE LIQUID VERSION

Excerpt from *Woman's World,* December, 1930.

Wassail or "wass hael" means "be of good health." This was a common expression of well-being at festivities, especially those associated with Christmas. The old-time wassail bowl overflowed with spiced ale or wine sweetened and flavored with cinnamon, cloves, roasted apples, etc., and was sometimes called "lamb's wool" or "King's Cup."

KING'S CUP

3 cups sugar

2 cups water

Thinly peeled rind of 2 oranges and 2 lemons

4 cloves

2 quarts cider (non-alcoholic)

1 inch cinnamon stick

Juice of 6 oranges and 6 lemons

1 quart ginger ale

Boil the sugar and water to a syrup with the orange and lemon rind, cloves, and cinnamon. Cool; strain into the orange and lemon juice and chill. Just before serving, add the cider and ginger ale.

Note: Prohibition in the US forced the editor to substitute ginger ale for the traditional wine and to ignore the custom of floating in it baked apple halves drenched with brandy that could be easily ignited.

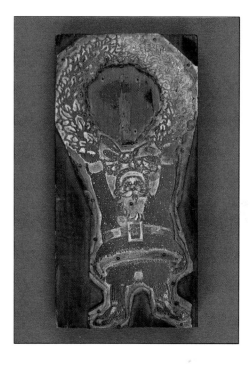

RIGHT
A printing block used for newspaper advertisements.

Banks and savings institutions shared the Christmas spirit by offering their customers Christmas Clubs to help them save money for the holiday. They advertised these clubs and other services on "Santa Claus Cards". Sometimes there were giveaways to customers who opened a club. These were often small banks with a holiday theme and were made of anything from cardboard to metal. Even the passbooks from the clubs often featured a Santa on the cover. All of these items are sought by collectors today.

The Christmas spirit has been present from the Magi at the Nativity to Scrooge in Dickens' *A Christmas Carol* to George Bailey's friends in *It's a Wonderful Life* and it will continue to be the cornerstone of the holiday.

CHAPTER TEN

To The Collector

WHERE DO YOU FIND THESE CHRISTMAS TREASURES?

The ideal location for Christmas ornaments and decorations, in the eye of the collector, is in the family attic. Not only is the age assured, but the finds have the sentimental value of family possession. However, most of us are not fortunate enough to find this trove.

A possible source close to home might be a neighbourhood garage or car boot sale. People sometimes sort through their Christmas decorations and put older items on the table for low prices. Bags of ornaments may contain one or two special finds. If there is a large box marked "Christmas", dig to the bottom. Paper decorations are a frequent sale item and might even include some rarity. Another "discarded treasure" is the feather tree. With its branches bent and twisted, it is sometimes a bargain. Of course, collectors must know what they are looking at, or what appears to be a bargain could be a waste of money.

Flea markets are always a good bet. Dealers spend much time

ABOVE
Japanese cotton batting Santas suspended by tinsel to create tree ornaments (1900 – 1930).

searching for and buying merchandise. A weekly market can be a magnet drawing the shopper back again and again, but sometimes holiday items are overpriced because the seller lacks specialized knowledge.

House auctions are the primary locations for adding to a collection. Relatives can sometimes confirm authenticity and the age of interesting items, but always remember that "What you see is not always what you get". Careful inspection and educated scrutiny before the sale can protect the collector from irreparably damaged ornaments or a reproduction Santa. Auction fever is the greatest danger of all. Trapped in the bidding spirit, you may soon find your wallet has been emptied. A knowledge of price ranges for the items and a willingness to set limits at the start of the auction can sometimes protect you (a friend pinching your arm can also help).

Antique shops and shows are another place for finding new additions to a collection. A dealer specializing in antique holiday decorations will frequently be an excellent source of information and hard-to-find items. The specialist is more likely to stock only authentic merchandise and may be willing to verify your purchase for a fee, but ultimately the collector must rely on knowledge of styles, fabrication techniques and market prices.

HOW DO YOU
KNOW WHAT YOU HAVE?

SANTA CLAUS In this speciality there are innumerable reproductions being sold as antique. The traditional German Father Christmas can be newly fabricated using the original moulds. These are very difficult to distinguish from the old, but there are a few tricks. A keen sense of smell is a good detector in sniffing out reproductions. The real antique Father Christmas will smell musty,

ABOVE
Santa dolls. (Left to right) Back row: Santa has a stuffed body, silky suit, composition boots and a moulded buckram face (1920s). A composition doll with movable arms, legs and head, wearing a cotton flannel suit (1930s). A plush acrylic-bearded and suited Santa with a plastic face; when this Santa is rocked, he produces music (1960s).

Front row: German plastic Santa that walks when the string attached to his belly is pulled (1950s). American "Roly Poly" musical Santa with plush acrylic suit (1950s to 1960s). Tiny American hard plastic Santa in a cotton suit with sleep eyes (1960s).

Asbestos concrete, three-dimensional torso of Santa Claus used for a rooftop decoration on a church parish house in the 1940s – 90cm (3ft) high.

RIGHT
These cardboard Santas were distributed to customers when they opened a Christmas Club Account (1940 – 1960). They are very collectable and are frequently used as tree ornaments.

ABOVE
Two examples of cast-iron Santas used to defraud the Christmas collector. Figures of this type appeared in antique shops and auctions in the US in 1985.

especially in the hollow inside. This is a very difficult smell to fake. If possible, do a side-by-side comparison with a confirmed antique Father Christmas. These figures are nearly a century old. Indicators of age like chipping, flaking, fading and decades of dust should be present, but they can be artfully duplicated.

Beware of a metal Santa Claus. Nearly all hollow and solid cast-iron figures have been reproduced. Cast-iron reproductions have been manufactured for so long that the earliest are old enough to complicate identification. Soft metal and tin can also be easily made to appear antique.

The definitive dating of metal pieces must probably be left to metallurgic analysis and experts. Some confidence can be gained in this area by familiarizing yourself with fabrication methods and techniques of assembly. Additionally, learning to tell the difference between true and false marks of ageing by observation can assist in identification.

Celluloid Santas are safe investments. The celluloid process has not been used since the early 1960s, so the chance of reproduction is slim. Celluloid was either marked with a sticker, or the company or country of origin was engraved in the mould. The latter mark can usually be found near the base of the Santa or on his back and is easy to find because it is raised from the surface. Celluloid Santas were produced in Germany, Japan and the United States. The products that were marked with paper labels are impossible to identify if the label is gone. Two prominent trademarks are "Irwin, USA", from the Irwin Company, and the "turtle" used by the German company, Rheinische Gummi und Celluloid Fabrik.

The composition Santa or Santa face was produced in Germany and Japan. The Santa figure is sometimes easy to identify merely by looking at the base where it is stamped. If the stamp is absent,

RIGHT
A contemporary glass ornament produced in West Germany. Ornaments of this type are often presented as antique.

the collector could compare the painted facial features. The German Santa will have precise features in flesh colours, while the Japanese Santa face will be bright pink. This is an accurate identification tool whether the composition face is on a cotton batting or chenille figure.

"Egg carton" papier-mâché Santas were predominantly produced in the United States and were usually unmarked. It is difficult to date these pieces. Style of clothing can give clues; the earlier figures have longer coats. More recent Santas are moving closer to the "universal image" as projected by Coca-Cola.

RIGHT
German blown glass ornaments (1920 – 1940). (Top row) Cockatoo with spun glass tail – 11cm (4¹/₂in); peacock – 7.5cm (3in); owl – 8.5cm (3¹/₂in). (Middle row) Peacock – 11cm (4¹/₂in); unsilvered red lacquered bird cage – 6cm (2¹/₂in); silvered cockatoo – 7.5cm (3in). (Bottom row) Songbird – 7.5cm (3in); birdcage – 7.5cm (3in); songbird with unusual black trim – 7.5cm (3in).

BELOW
Icicles. (Clockwise from lower left corner) Twisted lacquered metal – 12.5cm (5in) long (1920 – 1940); 1950s plastic – 12.5cm (5in) long; silvered blown glass – 8.5cm (3¹/₂in) long; and two styles of glass icicles (1910 – 1940) 5cm (2in) and 10cm (4in) long.

ORNAMENTS The thick glass wall of the kugel makes the difference between this and any other glass ornament obvious. The ornate brass or lead cap is tight and attached with a putty-type glue. The cap has a curved handle around which a ring is fastened. Reproduction of kugels is not known.

Occasionally lighter, unsilvered balls that have the same brass cap are confused with kugels, but again the difference is the weight. These small ornaments in a variety of simple shapes represent the transition from kugels to glass figural ornaments.

By the last quarter of the 19th century, the ornament industry's skill created the thin-walled ornament. If a collector purchases a box of ornaments at an auction, there are some guidelines to help pinpoint their age. An unsilvered ornament

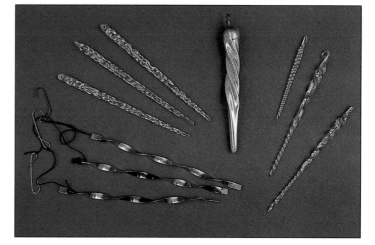

LEFT
German cotton Father Christmas with a scrap face, felt boots and a Dresden clasp on his robe (1900 – 1910). 30cm (12in) high.

with gold-painted highlights wrapped in lametta wire is probably a Victorian ornament and can roughly be dated as turn of the century. Popular shapes the collector might discover are barrels, parasols, baskets, balloons, or sailing boats. Fabric flowers or pieces of scrap can further clinch the date. These unsilvered ornaments are not reproduced.

If the auction box contains silvered glass ornaments, they could date from 1900 to the present. One obvious rule in dating is "If it looks new, it probably is" – age shows. The colour of the earlier ornament will have dulled slightly. There might also be crazing or cracks in the surface lacquer. By lifting the cap, the neck of the ornament can be observed. The silvering on the interior and neck can oxidize and turn black.

A subtle, more difficult clue is that older ornaments appear to be made of lighter glass when gently tapped. The lacquered surface of newer ornaments is, in contrast to old, extremely smooth. Additionally, the use of applied details such as rough or sanded trim is found more frequently on newer ornaments.

ABOVE
*German goose feather
tree from the 1920s,
14in. (35cm) high.*

The cap is another key to ornament identification. The problem, however, is the fact that the caps are easily removed. Since the caps are not directly connected, it is easy to put an old cap on a new ornament. The early metal cap is cut from soft metal. The metal tabs are folded over the glass neck and the wire spring is inserted through a slit.

The next design is a fully formed manufactured cap. This cap is round with an edge made to fit the neck of the ornament. The opening for the spring is part of the original shape.

Some knowledge of history and a magnifying glass will help identify an ornament. The ornament cap can be stamped with the name of the manufacturing country. For instance, a cap stamped "West Germany" is post-World War II, while the mark "Germany" is earlier than 1939.

An unsilvered ornament with a paper cap was undoubtedly produced during World War II in the United States. Occasionally a paper cap will surface on a silvered ornament. This is because the manufacturers continued silvering while the supplies still existed.

Cotton batting ornaments and trim need a word of caution. Ornaments are sometimes made today from "old" cotton batting utilizing "old" designs.

FEATHER TREES Feather trees are difficult to date. The new trees are made exactly like feather trees from 1915. The collector must again rely on "signs of ageing" such as dust, faded colours, or chipping on the composition berries. The style of the wooden base can be a clue to the age of older trees. Round turned-wood bases held early feather trees while square bases appear later. By the 1930s the country of origin might be stamped on the base of the tree.

A village scene created with German wood and paper houses and red and green brush trees (1930s). The centrepiece is a German two-tiered cityscape with trees, mica snow and a Dresden guardian angel (1910).

BELOW
A tabletop decoration made with contemporary crystal fir trees and antique German blown glass deer (1910 – 1940).

HOW DO YOU STORE YOUR COLLECTION?

The greatest dangers to the Christmas collection are heat and humidity. Fluctuating and high or low temperatures cause materials to degrade and surfaces to craze, chip and disintegrate. Moisture and humidity dissolve lacquers and paints and allow mildew to destroy. A dry, even temperature will greatly extend the life of a collection.

A second area of danger is chipping and abrasion. Objects banging or rubbing together are quickly damaged. Wrapping decorations in paper that can scratch or sand delicate surfaces will lead to great disappointment.

LEFT
A stereograph card with children peeking through the keyhole at Santa (1910).

To avoid these problems, use soft cloth such as old sheets; it is the ideal wrapping. Divided cartons make storage easier and safer. Small items fit in egg cartons and larger ones can be put in cartons designed for bottles. Other divided boxes can be found.

Another way of damaging and destroying fragile glass ornaments is to store them with hangers or wires attached. Inevitably, these sharp pieces of metal will scratch or pierce the ornament wall. While it is a time-consuming job, remove all hangers before wrapping and boxing.

CAN THIS BE CLEANED OR REPAIRED?

Unless you choose to live with obvious damage, additions to a collection should always be purchased in good condition. Some cleaning is possible on some items, but as a general rule light dusting with a clean, soft paint brush is as much as can be done.

Water is the great destroyer of Christmas decorations. Celluloid and plastic and some bisque can be washed with mild soap and cool water. Take care that water getting into the inside does not drip out and ruin a table surface.

Some minor restoration work can be done on non-glass items that have chips or cracks. Fill the area with thin plaster or porcelain repair compound or wood filler. Smooth over the surface carefully. Artist's acrylic paints are ideal for colouring. They are water soluble, have a dull surface when dry, and provide perfect matches for colours that have faded.

Feather trees can be lightly vacuumed to remove dust. If the feathers are shedding, the life of the tree can be prolonged by several light coatings of hair spray.

Having come to the end of our journey together we wish you much enjoyment with your Christmas collection and good luck in finding that special treasure.

Selected Bibliography

Auld, William Muir. *Christmas Traditions.* New York: The Macmillan Co., 1931.

Bach, Jean. *Collecting German Dolls.* Secaucus, New Jersey: Lyle Stuart, Inc., 1983.

Baum, L. Frank. *The Life and Adventures of Santa Claus.* Indianapolis, IN: Bowen-Merrill Co. 1902.

Bradford, Roark. *How Come Christmas?* New York: Harper & Row Publishers, 1948.

Brenner, Robert. *Christmas Past.* West Chester, PA: Schiffer Publishing Ltd., 1985.

————. *Christmas Revisited.* West Chester, PA: Schiffer Publishing Ltd., 1986.

Buday, George. *The History of the Christmas Card.* London: Spring Books, 1964.

Capote, Truman. *One Christmas.* New York: Random House, 1982.

Chalmers, Irene and friends. *The Great American Christmas Almanac.* New York: Viking Studio Books, 1988.

Coleman, Dorothy S., Elizabeth A., and **Evelyn J.** *The Collector's Encyclopedia of Dolls.* New York: Crown Publishers Inc. 1968.

Dickens, Charles. *Christmas Stories.* Rahway, NJ: The Mershon Company Press, 1898.

Douglas, Lloyd C. *Home for Christmas.* New York: Grosset and Dunlap Publishers, 1935.

Favor and Novelties. Gas City, IN: L-W Book Sales, 1985.

Gardiner, Gordon and Morris, Alistair. *The Illustrated Encyclopedia of Metal Toys.* London: Salamander, London, 1984.

Gray, Nada. *Holidays: Victorian Women Celebrate in Pennsylvania.* Lewisburg, PA: Oral Traditions Project of the Union County Historical Society, 1983.

Haywood, Carolyn. *How the Reindeer Saved Santa.* New York: William Morrow & Co. Ltd., 1986.

Hillier, Bevis. *Greetings from Christmas Past.*

London: The Herbert Press Limited, 1982.

Irving, Washington. *Old Christmas.* New York: Dodge Publishing Company, 1875.

King, Constance. *The Encyclopedia of Toys.* New Jersey: Book Sales Inc., 1978.

Koppelman, Susan (ed.) *May Your Days be Merry and Bright.* Detroit, MI: Wayne State University Press, 1988.

Kunnas, Mauri. *Santa Claus and His Elves.* New York: Harmony Books.

Lane, Julie. *The Life and Legends of Santa Claus.* Harleysville, PA: Tonnis Production Inc., 1983.

Miall, Antony & Peter. *The Victorian Christmas Book.* London: J. M. Dent & Sons Ltd., 1978.

Miles, Clement A. *Christmas Customs and Traditions.* London: Dover Publications Inc., 1976.

Morrison, Colin. *Christmas in Ireland.* Dublin: The Mercier Press, 1989.

National Wildlife Federation. *Trees of Christmas.* Washington, D.C.: National Wildlife Federation, 1988.

Perkes, Alden. *The Santa Claus Book.* Secaucus, NJ: Lyle Stuart Inc., 1982.

Reader's Digest Book of Christmas. Pleasantville, NY: Reader's Digest Association Inc., 1973.

Rogers, Maggie and Hallinan, Peter R. *The Santa Claus Picture Book.* New York: E. P. Dutton Inc., 1984.

Sams, Ferrol. *Christmas Gift.* Atlanta, GA: Long Street Press, 1989.

Schiffer, Margaret. *Holidays, Toys and Decorations.* West Chester, PA: Schiffer Publishing Ltd., 1985.

Shoemaker, Alfred L. *Christmas in Pennsylvania.* Kutztown, PA: Pennsylvania Folklife Society, 1959.

Smith, Jeff. *The Frugal Gourmet Celebrates Christmas.* New York: William Morrow & Co. Inc., 1991.

Snyder, Phillip. *The Christmas Tree Book.* New York: Penguin Books, 1977.

————. *December 25th.* New York: Dodd, Mead and Co., 1985.

Stille, Eva. *Christbaumschmuck.* Nuremberg: Hans Carl, 1979.

Time-Life Book of Christmas. New York: Prentice Hall Press, 1987.

Van Allsburg, Chris. *The Polar Express.* Boston, MA: Houghton Mifflin Co., 1985.

Witmyer, Margaret & Kenn. *Christmas Collectibles.* Paducah, KY: Collector Books, 1987.

USEFUL ADDRESSES

The Golden Glow of Christmas Past
PO Box 14808
Chicago
IL 60614
U.S.A.

Hearts of Holly
(The Holiday Collector's Newsletter)
PO Box 105
Amherst
NH 03031
U.S.A.

The Ornament Collector
Rural Route #1
Canton
IL 61520
U.S.A.

Bronner's Wonderland
Christmas Lane
Frankenmuth
MI 48734
U.S.A.

PICTURE CREDITS

All the collectable items featured in this book come from the authors' collection with the exception of the following:

7, 84, 85, 101(b) Harry Rinker; 10 Hulton Deutsch Collection; 17, 18, 19, 20(r) Library of Congress; 24 The Coca-Cola Company; 43(r) Images Colour Library; 48, 49, 51, 52 Christmas Archives International; 65 Bildarchiv Preussischer Kulturbesitz.

While every effort has been made to acknowledge all copyright holders, we apologize for any omissions.